Gooseberry Patch Co.

A Country Store In Your Mailbox®

Country Friends®

Good ★ Times

COUNTRY FRIENDS

Come along for a joyride...
good times, good eats, good friends!

A Country Store In Your Mailbox®

Gooseberry Patch Co.
149 Johnson Drive
Department Book
Delaware, Ohio 43015

Copyright 1998, Gooseberry Patch
1~888052~27~9

Fourth printing, March 2001

How to Subscribe

Would You Like To Receive ®
"A Country Store In Your Mailbox"?
For a two-year subscription
to our Gooseberry Patch catalog
simply send...
$3.00 to:
Gooseberry Patch
149 Johnson Drive
P.O. Box 190, Dept. Book
Delaware, Ohio 43015

Contents

Treat yourself to a good friend.

♥ DITCH THE CHORES AND GO TO THE PARK WITH A FRIEND. TAKE ALONG A BAG OF POPCORN AND SHARE IT WITH THE BIRDS. THE VACUUMING WILL WAIT!

♥ TAKE A DAY TRIP WITH A GROUP OF OLD FRIENDS ON A TRAIN. PLENTY OF TIME TO CATCH UP, AND PLENTY OF PRETTY SIGHTS TO LOOK AT AS THE WORLD ROLLS BY.

CO. FRIENDS

...3 cups cocoa, 2 lbs. butter, 12 eggs...

recipes

♥ PICK UP THE PHONE AND CALL A BOSOM BUDDY WHEN YOU NEED A LIFT, A PAT ON THE BACK, SOME COMMISERATION OR A RECIPE FOR DOUBLE MACADAMIA FUDGE.

♥ FIND A FRIEND WHO LIKES THE SAME THINGS YOU DO; FROM A FELLOW OPERA FAN TO A BOWLING BUDDY, COMMON INTERESTS WILL FURTHER A FRIENDSHIP.

♥ BE ADVENTUROUS — TRY SOMETHING COMPLETELY NEW & OUT·OF·THE·ORDINARY AND TAKE A FRIEND ALONG FOR THE RIDE. SO WHAT IF YOU'RE THE ONLY 48·YEAR·OLDS IN YOUR TAE KWON DO CLASS?

Be a good friend.

♥ TAKE HER KIDS OFF HER HANDS FOR A DAY. KEEP THEM ALL DAY. AND NO FAIR BRINGING THEM HOME EARLY.

♥ WHEN SHE CALLS TO DESCRIBE IN DETAIL HER DREAM ABOUT MICHAEL BOLTON SITTING IN A TREE OUTSIDE HER KITCHEN WINDOW, GIVE HER YOUR UNDIVIDED ATTENTION. LISTEN RAPTLY.

♥ BAKE A BATCH OF THESE

BEST FRIEND BLACK BOTTOM CUPCAKES

and deliver them anonymously to her at the office:

FILLING

- 1 · 8 OZ. PKG CREAM CHEESE, SOFTENED
- 1/3 C. SUGAR
- 1/8 t. SALT
- 1 LG. EGG
- 1 C. SEMISWEET CHOCOLATE CHIPS

CUPCAKES

- 1·1/2 C. ALL PURPOSE FLOUR
- 1 C. SUGAR
- 1/4 C. UNSWEETENED COCOA POWDER
- 1 t. BAKING SODA
- 1/2 t. SALT
- 1/3 C. VEGETABLE OIL
- 1 T. WHITE VINEGAR
- 1 t. VANILLA EXTRACT
- 1 C. WATER

Preheat oven to 350°.

Prepare filling: In a small bowl, cream the cream cheese with sugar & salt. Add egg ~ beat well. Stir in chocolate chips and set aside.

Make cupcakes: In a large bowl, sift together flour, sugar, cocoa, soda & salt. Add oil, vinegar, vanilla & water. Beat well.

Spoon batter into cupcake liners, about 3/4 full. Drop a small dollop of filling on top of each cupcake. Bake 20 minutes. Cool on wire racks.

7

A good friend...

...Knows the importance of a really big piece of fudge cake.

...will try to figure out a way to help you fit into a bathroom stall with your wedding dress on!

...tells you when you have toilet paper on your shoe.

...will hold your hand in the top row of the stadium because you're afraid of heights.

ADMIT ONE TO NOSEBLEED SEC

The only thing to do is to hug one's friend tight and do one's job.

— EDITH WHARTON

COUNTRY FRIENDS™
EMERGENCY KIT

PAINT AN OLD SUITCASE OR TOOLBOX TO HOLD "EMERGENCY" SUPPLIES:

chamomile Tea

Chocolate Candy

Tissues

Fuzzy Slippers

Teddy for hugging

GOOD FOR 1 ERRAND
Coupons for casseroles, errands & chores

DELIVER YOUR KIT TO A FRIEND WHO NEEDS SUPPORT OR A HELPING HAND ~

that's what friends are for!

HELLO .... GIRLFRIEND CRISIS LINE ...

I'm blue..

THE CURE: SEND HER A HAPPY FACE BOUQUET

... A GIFT SO DOWN-RIGHT SILLY SHE'LL HAVE TO SMILE!

YOU WILL NEED:

* SMILING PHOTOS OF YOUR FRIENDS & FAMILY
* FUSIBLE WEBBING
* POSTERBOARD
* WOODEN CRAFT STICKS
* GLUE
* COLORED PENS
* EMBELLISHMENTS

1. MAKE A COPY OF THE SMILING FACES IN THE PHOTOGRAPHS, USING THE PHOTOCOPYING MACHINE OPTIONS TO ENLARGE THEM TO DESIRED SIZES. BLACK & WHITE IS FINE ～ COLOR IS FUN.

2. CUT OUT EACH FACE & MOUNT TO POSTERBOARD WITH FUSIBLE WEBBING FOLLOWING PACKAGE DIRECTIONS.

3. GLUE A WOODEN CRAFT STICK TO BACK.

4. EMBELLISH YOUR SMILING FACES WITH PENS, RIBBONS, FEATHERS, SEQUINS ～ THE MORE OUTRAGEOUS THE BETTER. ADD CROSSED EYES, BUCK TEETH, BIG EARS, WHATEVER ORNERINESS YOU CAN DREAM UP.

5. STICK MASKS IN A BOUQUET & DELIVER A SMILE!

HI!

The greatest pleasure I know is to do a good action by stealth and have it found out by accident.
— CHARLES LAMB

WHILE A FRIEND IS AT WORK, BUILD A JOLLY SNOWMAN IN HER YARD TO GREET HER AT DAY'S END!

TIE RED BALLOONS TO HER CAR DOOR WHILE SHE'S IN THE DENTIST'S OFFICE UNDERGOING ROOT CANAL.

Secret Little acts of friendship

PLANT A BUNCH OF BLOOMERS IN HER VEGGIE GARDEN FOR A SURPRISE.

WASH HER CAR WHILE ...SHE'S AWAY.

MAKE AN ANONYMOUS DONATION TO THE LOCAL ANIMAL SHELTER IN HER HONOR.

love ya

DROP AN 8"X10" GLOSSY OF HER FAVORITE MOVIE STAR IN THE MAIL TO HER ON HER BIRTHDAY (AUTOGRAPH IT YOURSELF WITH A MUSHY MESSAGE & "HIS" SIGNATURE)

SNEAK A JUST-BAKED BATCH OF HER FAVORITE COOKIES INTO HER DESK DRAWER AT WORK. BLAME IT ON AN UNLIKELY CO-WORKER.

Kate

MAKE SURE SHE GETS A LETTER FROM SANTA TELLING HER SHE'S BEEN A VERY GOOD GIRL THIS YEAR... WHO WOULDN'T BE GLAD TO HEAR FROM ST. NICK?

RAKE HER LEAVES OR SHOVEL HER SNOW BEFORE SHE GETS OUT TO DO IT.

Kindness under-cover

♥ Little gifts to make her smile ♥

DO A MAY BASKET THING—RING THE DOORBELL & RUN LIKE MAD—BUT DO IT IN THE MIDDLE OF WINTER WHEN FRESH FLOWERS ARE REALLY A TREAT!

SNEAK IN HER GARAGE & PUT SPARKLY STREAMERS ON HER BIKE'S HANDLEBARS.

MAIL YOUR FRIEND A $5 GIFT CERTIFICATE TO THE LOCAL ICE CREAM SHOP ... ANONYMOUSLY. (JUST HOPE SHE TAKES YOU ALONG!)

POT UP A TINY SPRUCE TREE & LEAVE IT ON THE PORCH JUST BEFORE CHRISTMAS.

LEAVE A BOOK YOU THINK SHE'D LIKE ON HER PORCHSWING. TIE ON A RED RIBBON SHE CAN USE AS A BOOKMARK.

SLIP IN AFTER DARK & PLANT A SCARECROW IN HER ROSEBUSHES.

MAKE A DINNER RESERVATION FOR HER AT A NICE RESTAURANT AND PAY FOR HER MEAL AHEAD OF TIME.

GIVE HER A COUPON BOOK FULL OF OFFERS FOR ERRANDS & HOUSEHOLD CHORES.

How Nice! You Shouldn't Have!

Kindness ♥ is ♥ never wasted.

— S.H. SIMMONS —

LEAVE AN E-MAIL MESSAGE FOR HER.

Girlfriend Secrets:

"I actually read the tabloid magazines at the grocery store check-out and sort of believe the alien stories. I told Vickie and she didn't even laugh." - Kate

"Mary Elizabeth & my hairdresser know for sure... my hair is not naturally red."

- Holly

REALLY RED

LIVING COLOR

"Oh, the stories I could tell!" -Spotty

Girlfriends know the dirt on each other.

A Secret's safe 'twixt you, me & the gatepost!

— ROBERT BROWNING

girlfriends' GUILTY Pleasure: ROCKY ROAD Fudge

MUG SHOTS 1235   4278   8291   5412   3290

OK, WE CONFESS. WE TOLD EVERYONE WE WERE GOING TO THE GYM. INSTEAD, WE DROVE STRAIGHT OVER TO KATE'S AND ATE THIS FUDGE RIGHT OUT OF THE PAN. (LET'S JUST KEEP THIS OUR LITTLE SECRET, EH, GIRLFRIEND?)

* 4 $4\frac{1}{2}$-ounce milk chocolate bars
* 3   c. miniature marshmallows
* 3/4 c. coarsely broken walnuts

PARTIALLY MELT CHOCOLATE BARS OVER LOW HEAT IN SMALL PAN. REMOVE FROM HEAT ⌣ BEAT SMOOTH. STIR IN NUTS & MARSHMALLOWS. LET COOL AND SNARF DIRECTLY FROM PAN ⌣ OR SPREAD IN BUTTERED 8" X 8" PAN, CHILL & CUT WHEN SET.

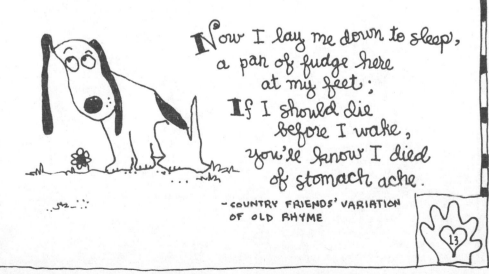

Now I lay me down to sleep,
a pan of fudge here
at my feet;
If I should die
before I wake,
you'll know I died
of stomach ache.

— COUNTRY FRIENDS' VARIATION
OF OLD RHYME

13

for Secret pals

★ Copy our little card below and tie it to a little gift for your secret pal!

Dear Secret pal:

You're my friend
I must confess
But who I am
You'll never guess!

A little gift from

...all's dear that comes from a friend.

~ HORACE

Time Flies.

"Yes'm, old friends is always best, 'less you can catch a new one that's fit to make an old one out of."

~SARAH ORNE JEWETT~

An old friend is a real pleasure.

No matter how long it's been since you've seen each other, you can pick up right where you left off....

You can remember her phone number from your junior high days....

She knows your little quirks and knows better than to put mayonnaise on your hamburger....

♥Do You♥ Remember?

These are a flash-back to years past... but why not encourage your children to revive the traditions?

Autograph Hounds

Bright canvas stuffed doggies bearing a ball-point pen record of all your childhood buddies~ ah, the memories!

Autograph Books

Little albums full of wise-cracks & flowery verse, authored by your very best friends... (just who was Cecilia B., though?)

Scrapbooks

Fat books stuffed with everything important: grade school report cards, science fair ribbons, photos of you & your friends on the swing sets... <u>so</u> many things to remember!

Tokens of friendship

♥Kindred Spirits Album♥

To commemorate a friend's milestone birthday ~or for no special occasion~ make a friendship gift she will treasure.

Give a group of friends the assignment of making a memory page or two ~ each person takes the blank paper and fills it with handwritten memories of the birthday girl. Photos, drawings, and mementos are especially-welcomed additions to the book~ whatever talents they can bring to the project are the special personal touches that will make the album a true treasure.

Gather everyones' finished pages and assemble in a pretty album~ or simply laminate each page and punch holes to bind with a beautiful ribbon.

...♥A very special gift of love!♥

17

Keep in touCH.

Mail a silly card for no special occasion.

Send extra prints of family photos to long-distance friends.

E·mail is easy.

Call a special bosum buddy every Sunday evening at 8. Keep the appointment!

Too busy to keep in touch with a group of old school chums? Try

Round Robin Letters

Write up a list of friends with their addresses. Now jot a letter out to the first friend on the list and mail it off. She will read your note, add her own news and send it on to the next old friend... and on it goes! The last person on the list sends the whole package back to you... and then it starts again.

Open the mailbox... Get ready for lots of gossip~ a long, long read awaits you!

Have an Old Friend Tea

summer '76

Brew up a good time with a group of old girlfriends!
Send out invitations that will set memories in motion:
photocopy an old photo of the whole gang and write
your party details under the picture. Encourage
your old friends to bring their photo albums and
yearbooks.

Set out a simple tea & dessert buffet,
and decorate the table with "remember when"
pictures and mementos. Spend an afternoon
reminiscing with old friends and enjoy!

(P.S. don't forget to provide disposable cameras for on-the-
spot updates for albums)

Old Friend Mint Tea

Take 5 or 6 stems of peppermint and spearmint from
your garden and place in a big metal pot. Add boiling water
to cover and let steep for several hours. Then use
this fragrant mint water to make your tea with regular
teabags ⤳ delicious and aromatic!

19

It's good to be just plain HAPPY.

So do the stuff that makes you happy. And do it with a buddy to double the fun!

* hit the after-Christmas sales and load up.

* go see a real tear-jerker at the theater and cry your mascara off.

Laugh it up.

* work on a garden project together.

Have a good giggle.

* dress up and go to a fancy restaurant.

BE SILLY together.

* go treasure-hunting together at the local antique shops.

Have FUN WITH A FRIEND.

* play a game, no matter how bad you are. Don't keep score.

* split a carton of Praline Chocolate Ice Cream and don't bother with dishes.

* yak for an hour or two.

Some of our **best friends** live right next door...

THANK your lucky stars for a great **neighbor**.

★ ♥ ★

TAKE A BIG PLATE OF WARM COOKIES & BOTTLE OF COLD MILK NEXT DOOR ON **September 28** AND TOAST TO YOUR FRIENDSHIP THAT IS **GOOD NEIGHBOR DAY.**

A little gift... to you from me

"Oh, how pleasant & sweet is the fruit which man hath planted & ordered with his own hand, to gather it & freely bestow it among kindred & friends." ~ R. AUSTEN

for a buddy from a country Friend's garden

Copy our flowerpot label and glue it on a plain old clay pot ... put in a handful of soil and a single bud from your flower-patch, for a sweet "remember me."

When friendship once is rooted fast,
It is a plant, no storm can blast.
–19TH century calling card verse–

to: _____

from your friend

↰ Copy & color if you like!

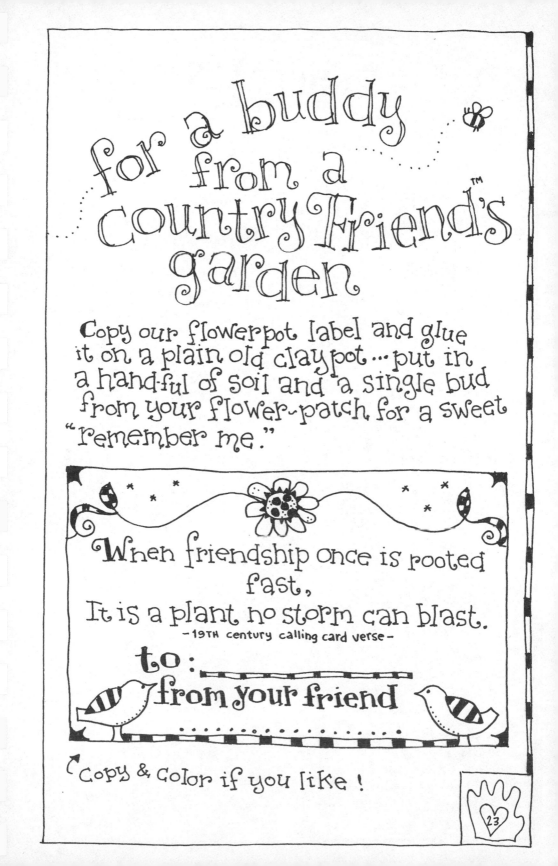

Make her CRY. (BUT A GOOD KIND OF CRY)

WRITE YOUR BEST FRIENDS A LETTER ~ BE UNABASHEDLY MUSHY ~ TELL WHY & WHAT YOU LOVE ABOUT 'EM.

REMEMBER THE DIFFERENCE SHE HAS MADE IN YOUR LIFE... and tell her so!

Make her LAUGH.

TELL OF THE FUNNY STUFF THAT BINDS YOUR FRIENDSHIP ~ THE TIME YOU GOT YOUR HAND CAUGHT IN A MAYONNAISE JAR & SHE HAD TO RESCUE YOU ~ THE TERRIBLE HOME-PERM YOU INFLICTED ON HER ~ THAT TRIP WHERE YOU BOTH GOT LOST AND HAD TO CALL HOME FOR DIRECTIONS BACK.

Dear Mary Elizabeth,
I just want to tell you what a wonderful friend you've been to me... no special reason, I don't have a disease or anything so don't go having a cow over me... well, actually that's one of my favorite things about you, you are always watching out for me and raving over how badly I eat... it's nice to have someone fuss over me! (BUT GET OFF MY BACK ABOUT THE CHOCOLATE, OK?) Ever since 3rd grade when you made Billy Evans quit picking on me at recess, you've been my protector. I think it's about time I told you thanks!
I also admire you for being such a good mother... you're kind to animals (especially old Spotty!)... and I also think you are especially graceful and

Tell her.

I like work; it fascinates me. I can sit and look at it for hours.
~ Jerome K. Jerome ~

★ BUNCHES ★ OF Country Friends™ ideas to Lighten the Load...

MARY ELIZABETH'S
SHORT-CUT TO HOUSEHOLD
HYGIENE:

K.I.S.S.

Keep It Short & Sweet

NOBODY WANTS TO SPEND HOURS, DAYS, WEEKS CLEANING HOUSE... TRY TO GET ORGANIZED & DO A LITTLE CHORE OR TWO EVERYDAY AND AVOID THE BIG CRUSH THAT INEVITABLY FALLS ON YOU IF YOU IGNORE 'EM DAILY. (BELIEVE ME, DUST BUNNIES MULTIPLY.)

So... START HERE.

The beginning is the most important part of the work.

— PLATO —
(427 – 347 B.C.)

I hate housework.

STEP 1
G.O.

Get Organized.

There's no time like the present to organize your household. Start here with these tips:

Keep a BIG
CALENDAR

RIGHT BY THE PHONE TO KEEP TRACK OF EVERYBODY'S APPOINTMENTS & SCHEDULES.

POST A
BIRTHDAY LIST

ON THE FRIDGE OF THIS MONTH'S SPECIAL DAYS.
(DON'T FORGET ANNIVERSARIES, TOO)

MAKE A
SHOPPING LIST

to save time & money. Keep it handy for all of your family members to write on it.

CHOCOLATE CANDY
CHOCOLATE CAKE MIX
CHOCOLATE ICE CREAM
COCOA
CHOCOLATE SYRUP
CHOC-COVERED PEANUTS
CHOCOLATE BROWNIE MIX
CHOCOLATE PUDDING
CHOC. MILK
CHOCOLATE FUDGE-SICLES

ORGANIZE A
SUPPLY BUCKET

To hold everything necessary to clean a particular room — and keep it stocked.

WRITE DOWN
GOALS
You set...
ANYTHING FROM CLEANING THE GARAGE TO ALPHABETIZING YOUR SPICES. NO GOAL IS TOO WEIRD.

You can't change my mind.

27

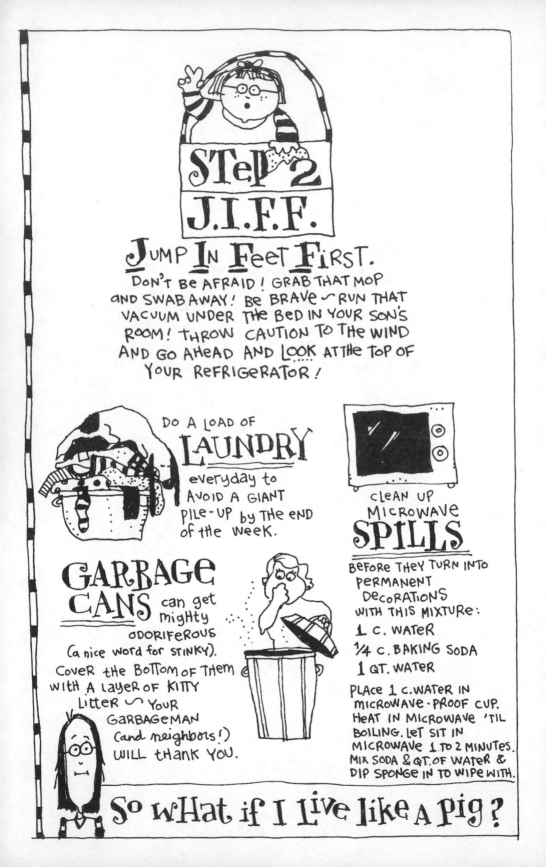

STEP 2
J.I.F.F.

JUMP IN FEET FIRST.

DON'T BE AFRAID! GRAB THAT MOP AND SWAB AWAY! BE BRAVE ~ RUN THAT VACUUM UNDER THE BED IN YOUR SON'S ROOM! THROW CAUTION TO THE WIND AND GO AHEAD AND LOOK AT THE TOP OF YOUR REFRIGERATOR!

DO A LOAD OF **LAUNDRY** everyday to AVOID A GIANT PILE-UP by THE END of THE week.

GARBAGE CANS can get mighty ODORIFEROUS (a nice word for STINKY). Cover the BOTTOM OF THEM WITH A LAYER OF KITTY Litter ~ YOUR GARBAGEMAN (and neighbors!) WILL THANK YOU.

CLEAN UP MICROWAVE **SPILLS** BEFORE THEY TURN INTO PERMANENT DECORATIONS WITH THIS MIXTURE:

1 C. WATER
1/4 C. BAKING SODA
1 QT. WATER

PLACE 1 C. WATER IN MICROWAVE-PROOF CUP. HEAT IN MICROWAVE 'TIL BOILING. LET SIT IN MICROWAVE 1 TO 2 MINUTES. MIX SODA & QT. OF WATER & DIP SPONGE IN TO WIPE WITH.

SO WHAT IF I LIVE LIKE A PIG?

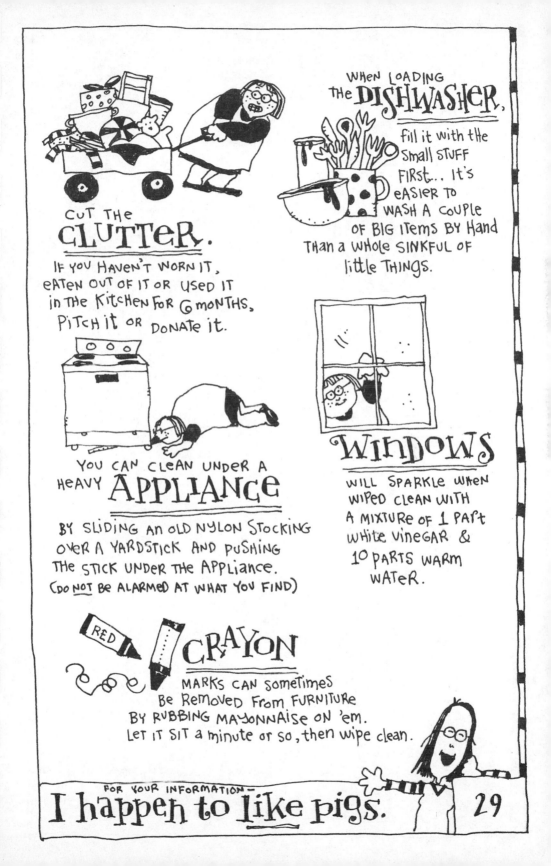

CUT THE CLUTTER.

IF YOU HAVEN'T WORN IT, EATEN OUT OF IT OR USED IT IN THE KITCHEN FOR 6 MONTHS, PITCH IT OR DONATE IT.

WHEN LOADING THE DISHWASHER,

fill it with the small STUFF FIRST... It's eASIER TO WASH A COUPLE OF BIG ITEMS BY hand than a whole SINKFUL OF little THINGS.

YOU CAN CLEAN UNDER A HEAVY APPLIANCE

BY SLIDING AN OLD NYLON STOCKING OVER A YARDSTICK AND PUSHING THE STICK UNDER THE APPLIANCE. (DO NOT BE ALARMED AT WHAT YOU FIND)

WINDOWS

WILL SPARKLE WHEN WIPED CLEAN WITH A MIXTURE OF 1 PART WHITE VINEGAR & 10 PARTS WARM WATER.

RED

CRAYON

MARKS CAN SOMETIMES BE REMOVED FROM FURNITURE BY RUBBING MAYONNAISE ON 'EM. LET IT SIT a minute or so, then wipe clean.

FOR YOUR INFORMATION—
I happen to like pigs.

REWARD YOURSELF WITH AN **ICE CREAM CONE**.

IT MAKES HOUSE-KEEPING SENSE: NO BOWL TO WASH.

STEP 3
F.W.A.T.

FINISH **W**ITH **A** **T**REAT.

AFTER A THOROUGH CLEAN-UP, BUY A BOUQUET OF FRESH FLOWERS TO **REVIVE THE SPIRIT**.

LAY DOWN ON THE CLEAN SHEETS AND TAKE A LITTLE **NAPPY-TIME** . (EVEN THE SHORTEST CHORE CAN BE EXHAUSTING)

★

Nothing adds to a person's leisure time like doing things when they are supposed to be done.

~ O.A. BATTISTA ~

I like the treat part!

Kitchen Karma

Is it your fate to spend hours in the kitchen? Let the Country Friends™ *enlighten you~* achieve culinary liberation with these shortcuts to household *harmony!*

PLAN AHEAD.

- Schedule one day a week to grocery shop.
- Mark favorite recipes in cookbooks with colored gummy stars or tabs for easy reference.
- Prepare a recipe like chili, soup or roast that can do double duty during the week.
- Fresh veggies can be prepared for cooking ahead of time. Wash, chop & refrigerate in water.

SIMPLIFY.

- Get rid of clutter.

KEEP KNIVES SHARP.

- A dull knife slows you down & adds more work.

I say call out for pizza.
THAT'S MY KARMA.

JoAnn's SPICY SHORT CUT STIR·FRY

A QUICK & EASY VEGGIE DISH SHE LOVES WITH CHICKEN!

*

2 T. UNSALTED BUTTER
1 RED BELL PEPPER, CHOPPED
1 T. MINCED JALAPEÑO CHILI
1½ t. GROUND CUMIN
1 16·oz. BAG FROZEN CORN KERNELS, THAWED
⅓ c. CHOPPED FRESH CILANTRO

*

MELT BUTTER IN HEAVY SKILLET OVER MEDIUM HEAT. ADD RED PEPPER & JALAPEÑO ~ STIR·FRY ABOUT 5 MINUTES. ADD CUMIN & STIR 30 SECONDS. ADD CORN & CILANTRO ~ STIR·FRY UNTIL CORN IS HEATED THROUGH.

Kitchen Karma

☆ short·cuts to household harmony

Learn to Love EASY DISHES.

—Like JoAnn's Stir·Fry (recipe at left) and other quick·to·prepare & quick·to·clean·up·after dishes.

— Don't be afraid to use convenience foods, especially when you can "embellish" them~ for instance, a boxed cake mix can be delicious with a homemade icing.

☆ CLEAN UP AS YOU GO.

—A little table salt poured on an oven spill will make it easier to clean up when the oven cools.
— A damp sponge makes a great spoon rest.

I wanna live in a HOUSE WITHOUT A KITCHEN.

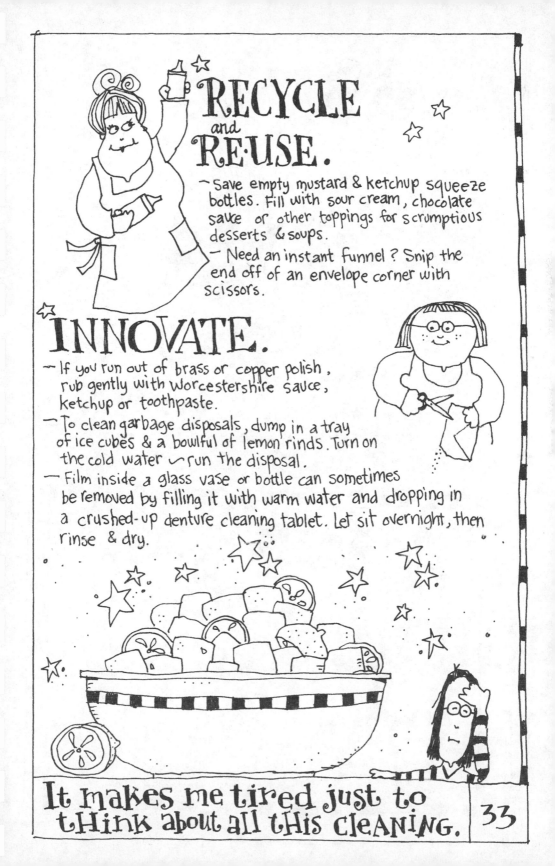

RECYCLE and RE·USE.

~ Save empty mustard & ketchup squeeze bottles. Fill with sour cream, chocolate sauce or other toppings for scrumptious desserts & soups.

~ Need an instant funnel? Snip the end off of an envelope corner with scissors.

INNOVATE.

~ If you run out of brass or copper polish, rub gently with Worcestershire sauce, ketchup or toothpaste.

~ To clean garbage disposals, dump in a tray of ice cubes & a bowlful of lemon rinds. Turn on the cold water ~ run the disposal.

~ Film inside a glass vase or bottle can sometimes be removed by filling it with warm water and dropping in a crushed-up denture cleaning tablet. Let sit overnight, then rinse & dry.

It makes me tired just to think about all this CLEANING.

33

JOB JAR

A great idea! Begin with a large clean jar or coffee can...make a copy of our label & glue it on...

JOB JAR

Take off the lid & reach right in... Choose a chore & then begin!

(and thanks for helping!)

Write chores on slips of paper...
let kids (and adults!) reach in for
a job!

Keep the chores simple so any
age can do the job:

- pull weeds in flower garden
- Set the table
- Empty trash in bathroom
- Wash Spotty's dish

And to keep it interesting,
slip in a bribe every now & then:

★ 1 free trip to Videoland
★ This coupon worth $1
★ redeem for ice cream cone
★ good for a hug & kiss

Some you win, some you lose.
～OLD SAYING～

- Clean toilet bowl
★ free trip to Super bowl

Very clever... BUT I DON'T
WANT TO PLAY, THANK YOU.

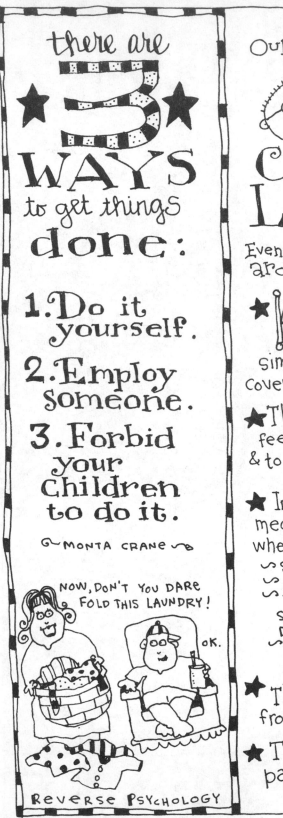

there are ★ 3 ★ WAYS to get things done:

1. Do it yourself.

2. Employ someone.

3. Forbid your children to do it.

~ MONTA CRANE ~

NOW, DON'T YOU DARE FOLD THIS LAUNDRY!

OK.

REVERSE PSYCHOLOGY

OUR SHORTCUTS:

CHILD LABOR

Even small·fries can help around the house:

★ They can make their beds~ it may be as simple as pulling the covers up to top of the bed.

★ They can learn to feed the family pets & to brush them, too.

★ Involve them in mealtime preparation when appropriate. They can:
- SET THE TABLE
- MENU SELECTION
- TOSS SALAD (PUT IT IN A SEALED PLASTIC BAG, ADD DRESSING & SHAKE)
- DUMP PRE-MEASURED ITEMS INTO RECIPES

★ They can sort socks from the laundry basket.

★ They can pick up papers & magazines.

CHORES for OLDER
K · I · D · S ·

VACUUMING

WASHING THE CAR

DUSTING

LITTERBOX PATROL

TRASH DUTY

Teach kids to put toys away at the end of the day. Set a certain time for pickup and play a certain song to help make the task more fun! (Remember Snow White & Mary Poppins)

BIRDCAGE MAINTENANCE

YARDWORK

PIANO MOVERS (JUST KIDDING)

Hey, I need some kids! A dozen or so will do.

Magical Vinegar

SHAZAAM! THIS HUMBLE HOUSEHOLD HELPER CAN WORK MIRACLES ALL OVER YOUR HOME!

★ Put a tablespoon or two of vinegar in your dishwasher to help cut grease.

★ Get rid of a stuffy, smoky smell in the kitchen by placing small bowls of vinegar around the room.

★ Remove wrinkles from clothing by using a pressing cloth dampened with diluted white vinegar.

★ Too many suds in the washer? Add ½ cup of vinegar to the rinse.

I look pretty good up there, huh?

Smellies be gone!

★ Stinky gym sneakers? Soak 'em overnight in a mixture of 1 part white vinegar to 3 parts water.

★ Before tossing perspiration-soiled laundry in the washer, spritz on a little vinegar.

★ To get strong odors off your hands, like gasoline, rub a bit of vinegar on them, then rinse.

Amazing!

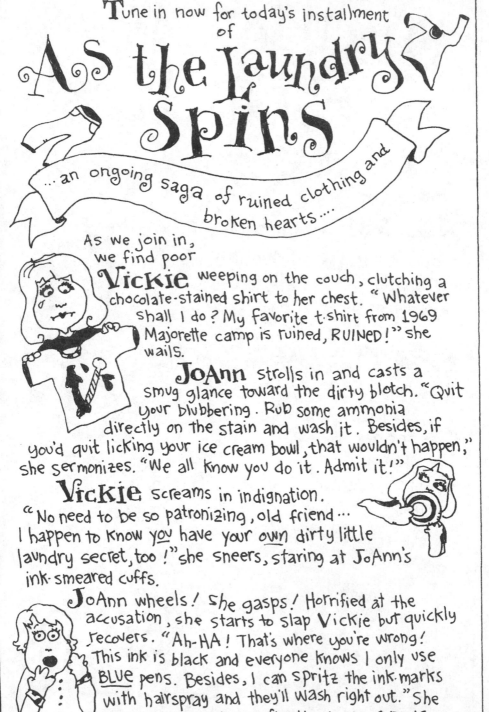

Tune in now for today's installment of

As the Laundry Spins

...an ongoing saga of ruined clothing and broken hearts....

As we join in, we find poor **Vickie** weeping on the couch, clutching a chocolate-stained shirt to her chest. "Whatever shall I do? My favorite t-shirt from 1969 Majorette camp is ruined, RUINED!" she wails.

JoAnn strolls in and casts a smug glance toward the dirty blotch. "Quit your blubbering. Rub some ammonia directly on the stain and wash it. Besides, if you'd quit licking your ice cream bowl, that wouldn't happen," she sermonizes. "We all know you do it. Admit it!"

Vickie screams in indignation. "No need to be so patronizing, old friend... I happen to know you have your own dirty little laundry secret, too!" she sneers, staring at JoAnn's ink-smeared cuffs.

JoAnn wheels! She gasps! Horrified at the accusation, she starts to slap Vickie but quickly recovers. "Ah-HA! That's where you're wrong! This ink is black and everyone knows I only use BLUE pens. Besides, I can spritz the ink-marks with hairspray and they'll wash right out." She paces nervously then defiantly shouts "PLUS— IT'S NOT EVEN MY SHIRT!" The End.

TUNE IN TOMORROW TO FIND OUT WHAT HAPPENS

WILL JOANN'S INK STAINS REALLY COME OUT? WILL HER HUSBAND SERVE HER WITH DIVORCE PAPERS FOR RUINING HIS FAVORITE SHIRT?

WILL VICKIE HAVE TO THROW AWAY HER BELOVED ANTIQUE T-SHIRT? WILL PSYCHIATRIC HELP DO THE TRICK?

Is JoAnn THE LOVE-CHILD OF JUAN PERÓN & EVA GABOR?

AND! In Past Episodes:

KATE'S NICE WHITE SHIRT TURNED INTO A NICE TAN SHIRT: SHE DYED IT IN COFFEE TO COVER THE COFFEE STAIN! SHE WORE IT AND NOBODY KNEW OF ITS SORDID PAST.

MARY ELIZABETH GROUNDED THE KIDS FOR LEAVING CHEWED BUBBLE GUM ON THE COUCH BUT MANAGED TO REMOVE IT BY RUBBING PEANUT BUTTER ON IT.

HOLLY LEARNED TO USE COLOR-CODED LAUNDRY BASKETS FOR EACH FAMILY MEMBER. SHE SIMPLY FOLDS THE LAUNDRY & PUTS IT THE BASKETS, THUS AVOIDING THE EMBARRASSING CONSEQUENCES OF PUTTING HER NIGHTIES IN BUD'S UNDERWEAR DRAWER BY MISTAKE.

...Join us again for more TITILLATING tales OF Laundry Gone Wrong!

What's gonna happen?

Poor, poor Vickie.

Pet Dilemmas

Help.

SPOTTY COVERED WITH BURRS FROM A ROMP IN THE WEEDS? APPLY A FEW DROPS OF BABY OIL OR SHAMPOO TO THE BURRS TO SOFTEN THEM, THEN BRUSH THEM OUT.

TO KEEP SPOT & HIS CANINE CHUMS FROM DIGGING HOLES, CRUMBLE A TOILET-FRESHENER CAKE IN THE DIGGING PLACE ⁓ HE THINKS THEY STINK!

CATS DISLIKE THE SMELL OF LEMON, SO PUT A COTTON-BALL SOAKED IN LEMON EXTRACT INSIDE A TEA BALL & HANG IT WHERE YOU WANT TO KEEP KITTY AWAY FROM. REFRESH WITH NEW OIL WEEKLY.

SECURE TRASH-CAN LIDS WITH A STRETCHY BUNGEE CORD TO FOIL LATE-NIGHT SNACKING BY MARAUDING DOGS & RACCOONS.

SPRINKLE BAKING SODA IN THE CAT'S LITTERBOX BEFORE YOU ADD THE KITTY LITTER TO ENSURE ADDED ODOR PROTECTION.

I think I'm Allergic to mops & brooms.

SHORT·CUT:

How to Darn A Sock

in 3 easy steps

by Kate

1. GRASP ONE HOLEY SOCK (one with holes, not the blessed kind).

2. HOLD CAREFULLY OVER WASTEBASKET WITH THUMB & FOREFINGER.

3. WHILE RELEASING SOCK, SHOUT "DARN!"

NOW, THAT WASN'T TOO HARD, WAS IT?

On Judgment Day,
If God should say,
Did you clean your house
today?

I will say,
I did not.
I played with the
children,
And Forgot.

~ Sue Wall ~

... the most important short-cut of all!

CHAPTER 3:

Lickety-Split

TIME
REMAINING UNTIL
NEXT CARPOOL COMES
:02 MINUTES :11 SECONDS

"On the rampage and Off the rampage ~ such is life!"
~ CHARLES DICKENS ~

Country Friends™
Recipes
for the times you
can't take
your time...

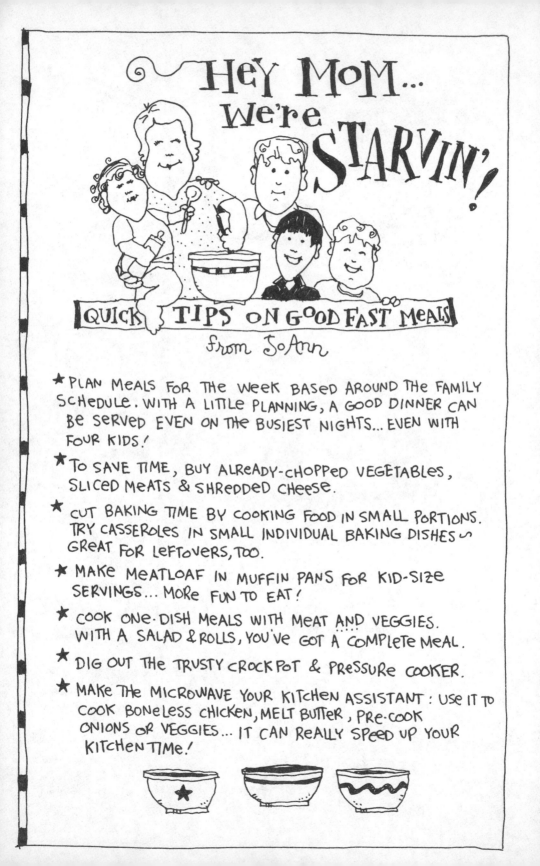

Hey Mom... We're STARVIN'!

QUICK TIPS ON GOOD FAST MEALS

from JoAnn

★ PLAN MEALS FOR THE WEEK BASED AROUND THE FAMILY SCHEDULE. WITH A LITTLE PLANNING, A GOOD DINNER CAN BE SERVED EVEN ON THE BUSIEST NIGHTS... EVEN WITH FOUR KIDS!

★ TO SAVE TIME, BUY ALREADY-CHOPPED VEGETABLES, SLICED MEATS & SHREDDED CHEESE.

★ CUT BAKING TIME BY COOKING FOOD IN SMALL PORTIONS. TRY CASSEROLES IN SMALL INDIVIDUAL BAKING DISHES ∽ GREAT FOR LEFTOVERS, TOO.

★ MAKE MEATLOAF IN MUFFIN PANS FOR KID-SIZE SERVINGS... MORE FUN TO EAT!

★ COOK ONE-DISH MEALS WITH MEAT AND VEGGIES. WITH A SALAD & ROLLS, YOU'VE GOT A COMPLETE MEAL.

★ DIG OUT THE TRUSTY CROCKPOT & PRESSURE COOKER.

★ MAKE THE MICROWAVE YOUR KITCHEN ASSISTANT: USE IT TO COOK BONELESS CHICKEN, MELT BUTTER, PRE-COOK ONIONS OR VEGGIES... IT CAN REALLY SPEED UP YOUR KITCHEN TIME!

Make~Ahead MEATBALLS

⌐PERFECT FOR FREEZING 'TIL YOU NEED A QUICK POST-GAME DINNER!

3 EGGS, BEATEN
¾ C. MILK
3 C. SOFT BREAD CRUMBS
⅔ C. ONION, FINELY CHOPPED
3 LBS. LEAN GROUND BEEF *
    * FOR LOW-FAT MEATBALLS, USE
        GROUND TURKEY OR CHICKEN
SALT & PEPPER TO TASTE
1½ t. WORCESTERSHIRE SAUCE

Combine eggs & milk in a medium mixing bowl. Mix in remaining recipe ingredients. Shape into 1" meatballs. Bake in 2 shallow baking pans at 375° for 25 to 30 minutes. Cool. Place in a single layer on a cookie sheet. Freeze until firm. Divide frozen meatballs into 3 freezer containers. Seal closed, label ⌐ return to freezer. Makes about 72 meatballs.

Now, you're ready...
the following delicious recipes
use these meatballs!

FOR ALL YOUR DAYS PREPARE, AND MEET THEM EVER ALIKE;
WHEN YOU ARE THE ANVIL, BEAR —
AND WHEN YOU ARE THE HAMMER, STRIKE.
    —EDWIN MARKHAM

Quick Meatball Meals

...these recipes use the meatball recipe on the previous page!

HOME · RUN MEATBALL SUBS

Combine meatballs with a jar or can of pizza sauce. Heat on stove top. Spoon into Italian sub buns. Top with thin slices of mozzarella cheese. Place in 350° oven for 5 minutes or until cheese is melted.

NINTH · INNING MEATBALL STEW

...delicious with a loaf of hot bread!

24 oz. pkg. frozen stew vegetables
16 oz. can seasoned tomatoes
½ t. salt
1 t. instant beef bouillon
⅛ t. pepper
1 bay leaf
3/4 c. water
1 pkg. frozen meatballs

Combine ingredients in dutch oven. Heat to boiling. Cover & simmer about 40 to 45 minutes or until veggies are tender. Stir occasionally. Remove bay leaf before serving.

Yummy
SWEET & SOUR CURVEBALLS

SO GOOD, THEY'LL THROW YOU FOR A CURVE!

1 T. CORNSTARCH
½ C. BROWN SUGAR
14 OZ. CAN PINEAPPLE CHUNKS
1 T. SOY SAUCE
⅔ C. VINEGAR
1 PKG. MEATBALLS
1 LG. GREEN PEPPER, CUT IN CHUNKS

IN A LARGE SKILLET, COMBINE CORNSTARCH & BROWN SUGAR. STIR IN PINEAPPLE CHUNKS WITH SYRUP, SOY SAUCE & VINEGAR. STIRRING CONSTANTLY, COOK UNTIL MIXTURE COMES TO A BOIL & THICKENS SLIGHTLY. ADD 1 PACKAGE OF MEATBALLS. COVER & SIMMER 10 MINUTES. BE SURE TO KEEP STIRRING OCCASIONALLY TO PREVENT SCORCHING. ADD GREEN PEPPER CHUNKS ~ COOK ADDITIONAL 5 MINUTES. SERVE OVER HOT STEAMED RICE. SERVES 5.

GARDEN & TIME MEATBALLS

... For those out in the outfield, full of good stuff from Mother Earth!

2 T. MARGARINE
1 CLOVE GARLIC, MINCED
½ t. DRIED THYME LEAVES
1 C. FRESH MUSHROOMS, SLICED

4 c. ZUCCHINI, THINLY SLICED
1 PKG. MEATBALLS
½ t. SALT
⅓ c. PARMESAN CHEESE
2 TOMATOES, CUT INTO WEDGES

Thaw meatballs in microwave.
Combine margarine, garlic, thyme, mushrooms & zucchini in big skillet. Cook 5 minutes. Add meatballs then cover & simmer until meat is heated thoroughly & veggies are tender. Sprinkle on salt & cheese. Add tomatoes ~ cook 2 to 3 minutes with cover on.

49

KATE's Seasoned GROUND BEEF FOR THE FREEZER

GREAT FOR CASSEROLES & SOUPS! USE IN ANY RECIPE OR PREPARED MIX CALLING FOR GROUND BEEF ~ONE LESS STEP AT SUPPERTIME!

5 LBS. LEAN GROUND BEEF
1 3/4 C. ONION, CHOPPED
1/2 t. GARLIC POWDER

2 t. SALT
1 t. PEPPER

Combine ingredients in large skillet or dutch oven. Cook 'til meat is brown. Drain off fat. Spread crumbled meat mixture in two shallow baking pans. Cool 5 to 10 minutes. Place in freezer for one hour. Crumble partially frozen meat mixture into small pieces. Place in freezer bags or containers. (About 3½ cups to each bag equals about one pound ground beef). Seal & label. Keep no longer than 3 months.

COUNTRY FRIENDS™ CHILI BURGERS

NO BULL! THESE ARE GOOD!

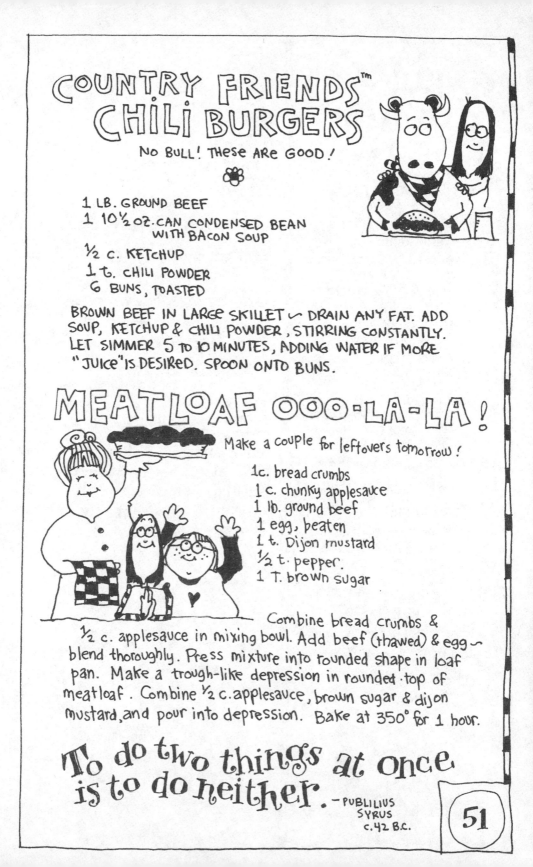

1 LB. GROUND BEEF
1 10½ OZ. CAN CONDENSED BEAN
   WITH BACON SOUP
½ C. KETCHUP
1 t. CHILI POWDER
6 BUNS, TOASTED

BROWN BEEF IN LARGE SKILLET ᴗ DRAIN ANY FAT. ADD SOUP, KETCHUP & CHILI POWDER, STIRRING CONSTANTLY. LET SIMMER 5 TO 10 MINUTES, ADDING WATER IF MORE "JUICE" IS DESIRED. SPOON ONTO BUNS.

MEATLOAF OOO-LA-LA!

Make a couple for leftovers tomorrow!

1 c. bread crumbs
1 c. chunky applesauce
1 lb. ground beef
1 egg, beaten
1 t. Dijon mustard
½ t. pepper
1 T. brown sugar

Combine bread crumbs & ½ c. applesauce in mixing bowl. Add beef (thawed) & egg ᴗ blend thoroughly. Press mixture into rounded shape in loaf pan. Make a trough-like depression in rounded top of meatloaf. Combine ½ c. applesauce, brown sugar & dijon mustard, and pour into depression. Bake at 350° for 1 hour.

To do two things at once is to do neither. —PUBLILIUS SYRUS c. 42 B.C.

51

the QUICK~ COOKER'S PANTRY

... GOT 'EM ?

- ☐ BROTH ~ BEEF & CHICKEN
- ☐ BOUILLON CUBES
- ☐ BREAD CRUMBS, REGULAR OR SEASONED
- ☐ CANNED TUNA & CHICKEN
- ☐ CANNED TOMATOES & TOMATO SAUCE, NO SALT & SEASONED VARIETIES
- ☐ CANNED BEANS
- ☐ CAKE & QUICK BREAD MIXES
- ☐ CONDIMENTS ~ SALSA, SOY SAUCE, HOT PEPPER SAUCE, HONEY, HORSERADISH, KETCHUP, MUSTARDS
- ☐ SOUP ~ CANNED & DRY MIXES
- ☐ PASTA ~ ALL SHAPES & SAUCES
- ☐ PEANUT BUTTER
- ☐ RICE ~ REGULAR, INSTANT & DON'T FORGET BROWN!
- ☐ OATMEAL
- ☐ SEASONINGS ~ HERBS, SPICES & GARLIC
- ☐ READY-MADE PASTA SAUCES
- ☐ WALNUTS, PECANS & ALMONDS
- ☑ CHOCOLATE CHIPS
- ☐ VINEGARS

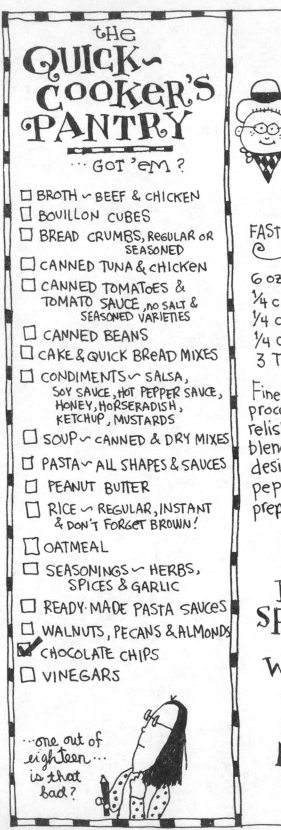

... one out of eighteen ... is that bad?

Hungry Kids Ham Spread

FAST TO MAKE ★ QUICK TO JUST DISAPPEAR!

6 oz. ham (about 1⅓ c. chopped)
¼ c. chopped celery
¼ c. onion (optional)
¼ c. mayonnaise
3 T. sweet pickle relish

Finely chop ham in food processor. Add celery, mayo & relish and mix just until blended. Add onion, too, if desired. Season with salt & pepper. Cover & chill. Can be prepared 1 day ahead.

2 HAM SPREAD on WHITE to GO, MOM!

EEK!

Company's coming and nobody bothered to tell the cook~namely

YOU.

No time for a meal but, if you can get away with an elegant dessert, we've got a few ideas that are quick.
And easy.
And not too messy.

So don't

PANIC.

... Just follow along. Quick!
→

PANIC-FREE DESSERTS

Pretend Chocolate Torte

IT'S CHOCOLATE. IT'S A TORTE. THE ONLY PRETEND PART IS PLAYING-LIKE IT TOOK HOURS & HOURS & HOURS TO PREPARE!

START WITH A PLAIN OLD CHOCOLATE CAKE MIX. BAKE ACCORDING TO BOX DIRECTIONS. (WHILE IT'S IN THE OVEN, HIDE ALL THE DIRTY DISHES INSIDE THE WASHING MACHINE). SPLIT COOLED CAKE LAYERS IN HALF. SPREAD RASPBERRY PRESERVES BETWEEN LAYERS. STACK IT BACK TOGETHER AND GLOB WHIPPED DAIRY TOPPING ON TOP. ADD FRESH BERRIES ON TOP IF YOU HAVE 'EM ⌣ IF NOT, PLOP A HANDFUL OF CHOCOLATE CHIPS ON THERE. VOILÁ!

Uncommonly Delicious Fruit Parfaits

HERE'S THE TRICK: IT'S PLAIN OLD FRUIT AND WHAT-HAVE-YOU SERVED IN A BEAUTIFUL WINEGLASS. THEY'LL THINK THEY'RE ROYALTY ⌣ YOU'LL KNOW IT'S JUST THE NEIGHBORS SNARFING UP BANANAS & VANILLA PUDDING.

FIND YOUR BEST WINEGLASSES OR EVEN PRETTY CLEAR GLASSES. GOT SOME VANILLA PUDDING, ICE CREAM OR YOGURT? WHATEVER YOU'VE GOT, SPOON IT IN THE GLASSES ⌣ JUST AN INCH OR SO. SLICE UP SOME FRUIT, CRUNCH UP SOME CHOCOLATE SANDWICH COOKIES, WHATEVER (PICKLE RELISH IS NOT A GOOD IDEA) ⌣ LAYER IT ON TOP OF THE VANILLA STUFF. NOW, JUST KEEP LAYERING IT 'TIL THE GLASS IS FULL. ELEGANT, HUH?

Zippidy·Doo·Dah Lemon Pie

ZIPPY & ZESTY, TAKES JUST A MINUTE TO FIX... WHAT MORE CAN A HARRIED HOSTESS ASK FOR?

3 EGGS, BEATEN TO A FROTH
JUICE OF 2 LEMONS, STRAINED
1 C. SUGAR
1 C. HEAVY CREAM
PREPARED GRAHAM·CRACKER CRUST
½ C. GRAHAM·CRACKER CRUMBS

COOK EGGS, LEMON JUICE & SUGAR IN A DOUBLE BOILER 'TIL JUST THICK, STIRRING CONSTANTLY. REMOVE FROM HEAT & ALLOW TO COOL TO ROOM TEMPERATURE. IN THE MEANTIME, WHIP CREAM WITHOUT SUGAR UNTIL PEAKS FORM, THEN FOLD INTO LEMON BASE. POUR MIXTURE INTO CRUST. TOP WITH GRAHAM·CRACKER CRUMBS. REFRIGERATE UNTIL SERVING TIME.

It is surely Later than you think,
It is certainly Later than you think,
It is definitely Later than you think,
It is undoubtedly Later than you think.

~ Merrill Moore ~

55

BREAKFAST SHAKE·UP

A YUMMY MEAL-IN-A-MUG-IN-A-MINUTE!

$\frac{1}{2}$ C. ICY COLD ORANGE JUICE
1 BANANA, SLICED
$\frac{1}{2}$ C. BUTTERMILK
$\frac{1}{4}$ C. VANILLA YOGURT

COMBINE ALL INGREDIENTS IN A BLENDER. PROCESS UNTIL THICK & CREAMY SMOOTH. SERVE IN A CHILLED MUG.

VARIATIONS: USE $\frac{1}{2}$ C. RIPE STRAWBERRIES
OR
2 PEACHES OR NECTARINES, PEELED, PITTED & CHOPPED

WAKE·UP!

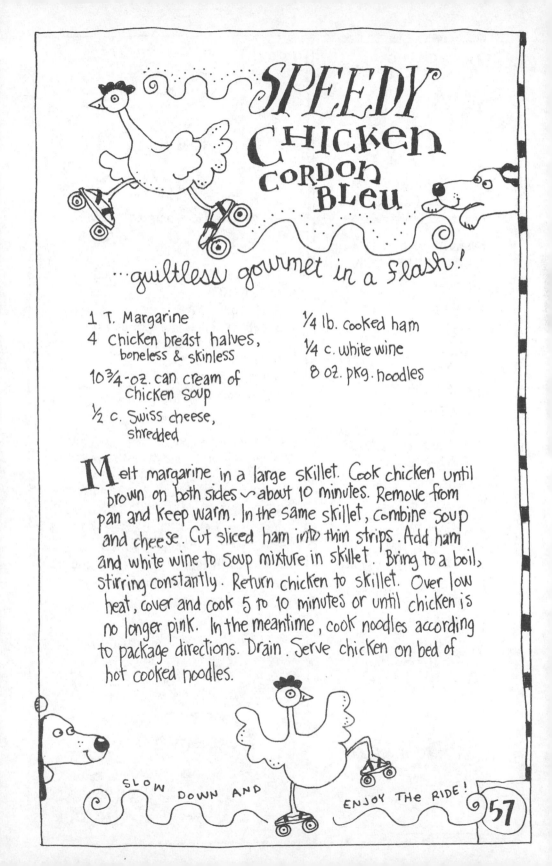

SPEEDY CHICKEN CORDON BLEU

...guiltless gourmet in a flash!

1 T. Margarine
4 chicken breast halves, boneless & skinless
10¾-oz. can cream of chicken soup
½ c. Swiss cheese, shredded

¼ lb. cooked ham
¼ c. white wine
8 oz. pkg. noodles

Melt margarine in a large skillet. Cook chicken until brown on both sides ‿ about 10 minutes. Remove from pan and keep warm. In the same skillet, combine soup and cheese. Cut sliced ham into thin strips. Add ham and white wine to soup mixture in skillet. Bring to a boil, stirring constantly. Return chicken to skillet. Over low heat, cover and cook 5 to 10 minutes or until chicken is no longer pink. In the meantime, cook noodles according to package directions. Drain. Serve chicken on bed of hot cooked noodles.

SLOW DOWN AND ENJOY THE RIDE!

THE QUICK-COOKER'S STAND-BYS:

STAPLES TO KEEP IN FRIDGE & FREEZER

- ☐ GROUND MEAT — LEAN BEEF, TURKEY & CHICKEN
- ☐ MEATBALLS
- ☐ MINI MEAT LOAVES
- ☐ FROZEN VEGGIES
- ☐ GRATED & SHREDDED CHEESE
- ☐ FRESH FRUIT
- ☐ FRESH VEGGIES — GREEN PEPPERS, ONIONS, CABBAGE, CARROTS, CELERY & BROCCOLI
- ☐ SALAD GREENS
- ☐ CORN & FLOUR TORTILLAS
- ☐ SOUR CREAM, NONFAT OR REGULAR
- ☐ FROZEN WHIPPED TOPPING
- ☐ FRESH HERBS — PARSLEY, CILANTRO, ROSEMARY, MINT, BASIL & DILL

EARLY A.M. French TOAST

— a make-ahead dish —

◆ ◆ ◆ ◆ ◆

1 c. BROWN SUGAR
½ c. BUTTER
2 T. CORN SYRUP
1 LOAF FRENCH BREAD, CUT INTO THICK SLICES
5 EGGS
1½ c. MILK
1 t. VANILLA EXTRACT

◆

In a medium saucepan over medium heat, mix & melt brown sugar, butter & corn syrup. Spray a baking dish with non-stick vegetable oil and fill with the butter mixture.

Mix eggs, milk & vanilla. Arrange bread slices in baking dish. Pour egg mixture over bread; don't miss any area — use all the mixture. Any extra will be soaked up by the bread.

Cover dish and refrigerate over-night. The next morning, simply uncover and slip into a 350° oven for 30 minutes, then serve.

WHO KNEW I COULD BE SO QUICK & DELICIOUS?

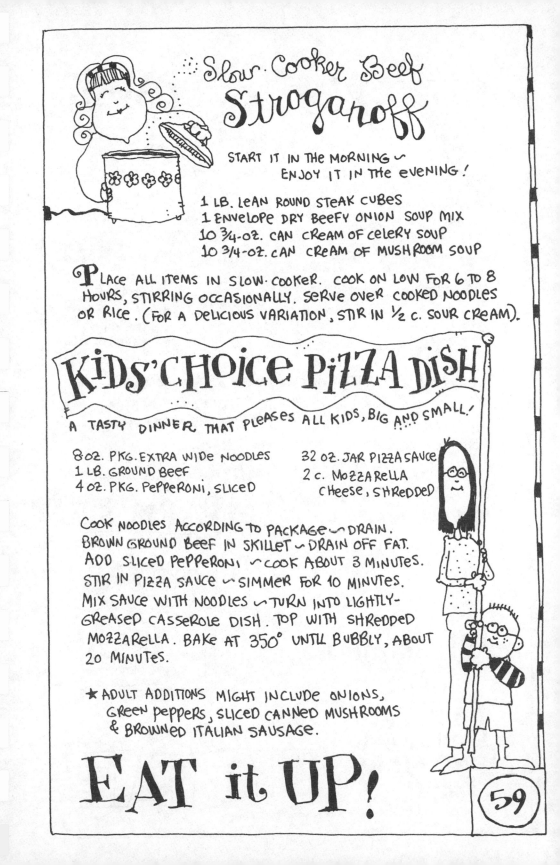

Slow Cooker Beef Stroganoff

START IT IN THE MORNING ~
ENJOY IT IN THE EVENING!

1 LB. LEAN ROUND STEAK CUBES
1 ENVELOPE DRY BEEFY ONION SOUP MIX
10 3/4-OZ. CAN CREAM OF CELERY SOUP
10 3/4-OZ. CAN CREAM OF MUSHROOM SOUP

PLACE ALL ITEMS IN SLOW-COOKER. COOK ON LOW FOR 6 TO 8 HOURS, STIRRING OCCASIONALLY. SERVE OVER COOKED NOODLES OR RICE. (FOR A DELICIOUS VARIATION, STIR IN 1/2 c. SOUR CREAM).

KIDS' CHOICE PIZZA DISH

A TASTY DINNER THAT PLEASES ALL KIDS, BIG AND SMALL!

8 OZ. PKG. EXTRA WIDE NOODLES
1 LB. GROUND BEEF
4 OZ. PKG. PEPPERONI, SLICED

32 OZ. JAR PIZZA SAUCE
2 c. MOZZARELLA CHEESE, SHREDDED

COOK NOODLES ACCORDING TO PACKAGE ~ DRAIN. BROWN GROUND BEEF IN SKILLET ~ DRAIN OFF FAT. ADD SLICED PEPPERONI ~ COOK ABOUT 3 MINUTES. STIR IN PIZZA SAUCE ~ SIMMER FOR 10 MINUTES. MIX SAUCE WITH NOODLES ~ TURN INTO LIGHTLY-GREASED CASSEROLE DISH. TOP WITH SHREDDED MOZZARELLA. BAKE AT 350° UNTIL BUBBLY, ABOUT 20 MINUTES.

★ ADULT ADDITIONS MIGHT INCLUDE ONIONS, GREEN PEPPERS, SLICED CANNED MUSHROOMS & BROWNED ITALIAN SAUSAGE.

EAT it UP!

Zippy Vegetable Casserole

MAKE IT AHEAD OF TIME & STORE
IN THE FRIDGE UP TO 24 HOURS... YUM!

3 c. Fresh plum tomatoes, seeded & chopped

3 c. zucchini, chopped

3 medium onions, chopped

3 cloves garlic, minced

¼ c. fresh parsley, minced

¼ c. fresh basil, finely chopped

1 c. mozzarella cheese, shredded

2½ c. bread crumbs

Coat a shallow baking dish with nonstick vegetable spray. Place tomatoes, zucchini, onions, garlic, parsley & basil in pan. Mix together cheese & bread crumbs. Toss 1½ c. of the crumb mixture with veggies. Sprinkle remaining crumbs over top of veggies. Refrigerate until ready to bake. Bake at 350° for about 55 minutes.

FARM FRESH

The time to Relax is when you don't have time for it.
~ Sydney J. Harris ~

Easy Oven Roast

CLEAN-UP IS A SNAP SINCE THE ENTIRE MEAL IS PREPARED IN A FOIL WRAPPER!

3 TO 4 LB. BEEF CHUCK ROAST
10 3/4-OZ. CAN CREAM OF MUSHROOM SOUP

1 ENVELOPE DRY ONION SOUP MIX
10 OZ. BOX FROZEN PEAS & CARROTS

Place roast on large piece of heavy-duty aluminum foil. Spread mushroom soup on top of roast. Sprinkle dry onion soup mix over soup-covered roast. Add frozen peas & carrots. Seal foil over roast tightly, and place in roasting pan. Cook in 300° oven for 3.½ to 4 hours. Open foil carefully to release steam. Soup makes a delicious gravy — perfect over rice, noodles or mashed potatoes.

The hard part is waiting to eat it!

Home ✦ Breads
IN A
✦ SNAP ✦

who's got time to make homemade bread? You do! Try our recipes!

EASY 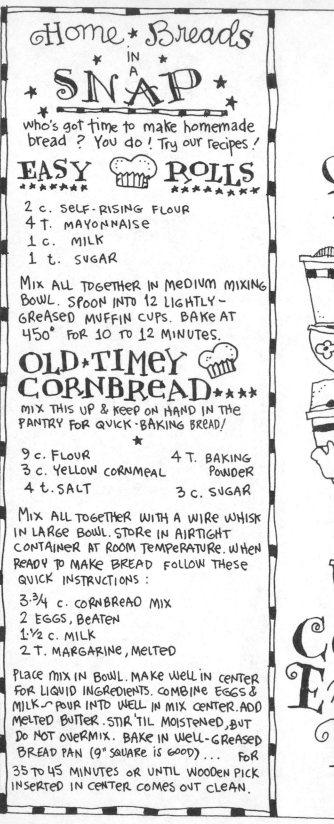 ROLLS
★★★★★ *★★★★★★★★★*

2 c. SELF-RISING FLOUR
4 T. MAYONNAISE
1 c. MILK
1 t. SUGAR

MIX ALL TOGETHER IN MEDIUM MIXING BOWL. SPOON INTO 12 LIGHTLY-GREASED MUFFIN CUPS. BAKE AT 450° FOR 10 TO 12 MINUTES.

OLD ★ TIMEY CORNBREAD ★★★

MIX THIS UP & KEEP ON HAND IN THE PANTRY FOR QUICK-BAKING BREAD!
★

9 c. FLOUR
3 c. YELLOW CORNMEAL
4 t. SALT
4 T. BAKING POWDER
3 c. SUGAR

MIX ALL TOGETHER WITH A WIRE WHISK IN LARGE BOWL. STORE IN AIRTIGHT CONTAINER AT ROOM TEMPERATURE. WHEN READY TO MAKE BREAD FOLLOW THESE QUICK INSTRUCTIONS:

3·3/4 c. CORNBREAD MIX
2 EGGS, BEATEN
1·1/2 c. MILK
2 T. MARGARINE, MELTED

PLACE MIX IN BOWL. MAKE WELL IN CENTER FOR LIQUID INGREDIENTS. COMBINE EGGS & MILK ~ POUR INTO WELL IN MIX CENTER. ADD MELTED BUTTER. STIR 'TIL MOISTENED, BUT DO NOT OVERMIX. BAKE IN WELL-GREASED BREAD PAN (9" SQUARE IS GOOD) ... FOR 35 TO 45 MINUTES OR UNTIL WOODEN PICK INSERTED IN CENTER COMES OUT CLEAN.

You are invited to a Country Friends™

Casserole Exchange Party

WHAT YOU NEED TO BEGIN:

* 3 TO 5 GOOD BUDDIES
* SEVERAL HOURS OF UNINTERRUPTED TIME
  (I.E. NO KIDS OR HUSBANDS UNDERFOOT)
* 1 KITCHEN

ASK EACH FRIEND TO BRING:

* A FAVORITE CASSEROLE RECIPE WRITTEN OUT ON RECIPE CARDS
* COMPLETE INGREDIENTS FOR THE CASSEROLE TIMES THE NUMBER OF PARTY GUESTS
* ALUMINUM CASSEROLE DISH FOR EACH GUEST

THE GOAL:

* EACH GUEST SHOULD GO HOME WITH 3 TO 5 CASSEROLES FOR THE FREEZER!

HINTS FOR A FUN PARTY:

DIVIDE THE WORK AMONG FRIENDS ✓ LET KATE CHOP, SET HOLLY TO STIRRING.... TRY THE ASSEMBLY LINE METHOD FOR PUTTING THE CASSEROLES TOGETHER.

GIVE EVERY GUEST A CHEF'S HAT OR APRON. YOU CAN BUY INEXPENSIVE PAPER VERSIONS OR GIVE NICE FABRIC ONES ✓ AN ENTICEMENT TO WEAR THEM AGAIN AT THE NEXT PARTY.

THIS GET-TOGETHER IS ESPECIALLY NICE WHEN IT'S FOR A GOOD CAUSE:
* A NEW MOM OR SOMEONE JUST HOME FROM THE HOSPITAL
* AN ELDERLY PERSON * A NEW NEIGHBOR WELCOME
* SOMEONE WHO'S MOVING

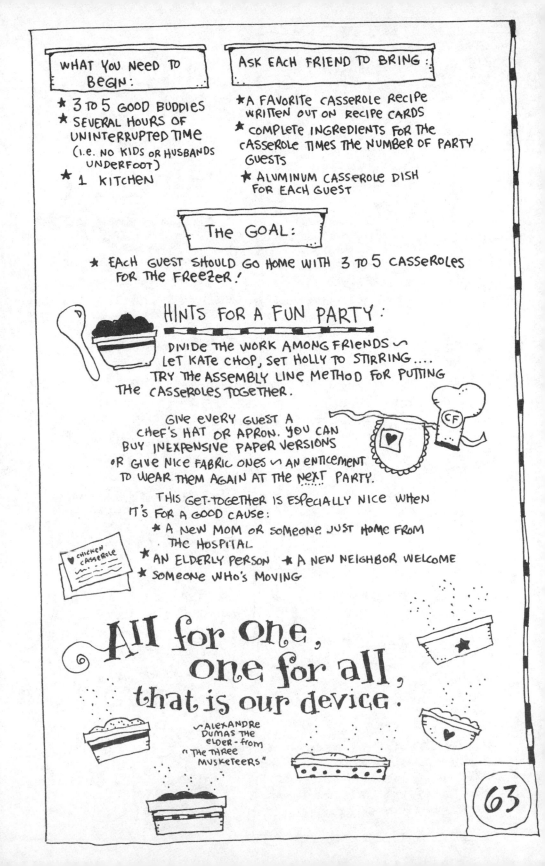

All for one, one for all, that is our device.

✓ ALEXANDRE DUMAS THE ELDER - FROM "THE THREE MUSKETEERS"

THE COUNTRY FRIENDS™ ♥ABSOLUTE♥ Favorites

QUESTION: what would be your favorite quickie meal if you don't have to feed anyone but your self?

★

HOLLY ♥: I'd open a can of Beluga caviar, and imported sesame crackers with champagne to wash it down.

KATE ♥: Triple Big Smacky Burger with cheese and anchovies, hold the ketchup, from the drive-thru window at Uncle Greasy's.

VICKIE ♥: A cup of tea and a half-dozen oatmeal cookies... big ones.

JOANN ♥: A bag of extra-salty pretzels and a bologna sandwich, please, with a malt.

MARY ELIZABETH ♥: Just hand me that box of left-over peanut brittle and I'll be fine.

★

(PUBLISHER'S NOTE: THE ABOVE SO-CALLED MEALS ARE NOT SANCTIONED BY THE MANAGEMENT, AND REPEATED INTAKE OF SUCH MAY RESULT IN HEART DISEASE, BRAIN DAMAGE & FAT THIGHS.)

SPOTTY'S SPEEDY SPANISH SKILLET

...a one-pan wonder!

1 small green pepper, cut in strips
1 T. butter
2 15-oz. cans Spanish rice
12 oz. can whole kernel corn, drained
1½ t. minced dried onion
3/4 c. canned black beans, rinsed
16 oz. can Mexican-style tomatoes, chopped

½ t. Worcestershire sauce
dash ground red pepper
few dashes of hot sauce
3/4 c. sharp Cheddar cheese, grated

*

Cook green pepper in butter until tender. Stir in remaining ingredients except cheese. Heat through. Sprinkle cheese on top just before serving.

¡ole!

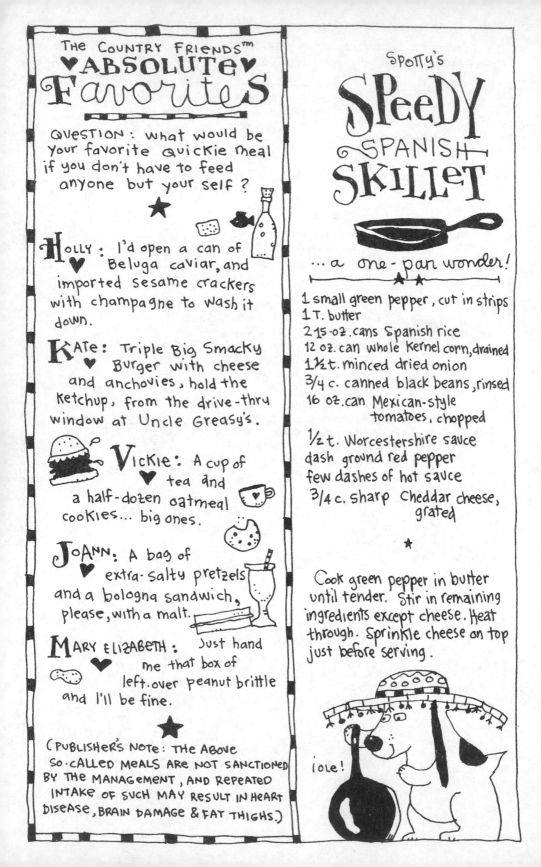

Pork chops
à la Holly

...perfectly pulchritudinous!

...just a lovely casserole to prepare early and eat later.

...delicious!

6 lean pork chops
3/4 c. raw rice
1 lg. onion, sliced
6 thick slices of tomato
   or 2 c. canned tomatoes

1 lg. green pepper, sliced into rings
1 c. beef broth
1 c. tomato juice
1/8 c. thyme leaves
1/8 c. marjoram leaves

Brown chops in skillet. Salt & pepper to taste. Place rice in bottom of a lightly greased casserole or pan — the dish should be fairly large. Place a slice of onion on each chop, followed by a tomato slice or 1/3 c. canned tomatoes. Finish topping with a green pepper ring. (At this point, casserole may be covered and placed in refrigerator until later.) Add beef broth & tomato juice to skillet. Stir in thyme & marjoram. Simmer 10 minutes. Place in separate container in refrigerator. When ready to bake casserole, pour liquid over chops & rice. Cover & bake at 375° for 1 hour. Serves 6.

No man is useless while he has a friend.
— ROBERT LOUIS STEVENSON —

NO FRIEND IS USELESS WHEN SHE COMES BEARING PORK CHOPS. — SPOTTY

Country Friends™
PASTA DELIGHT
...SIMPLE & SIMPLY marvelous!

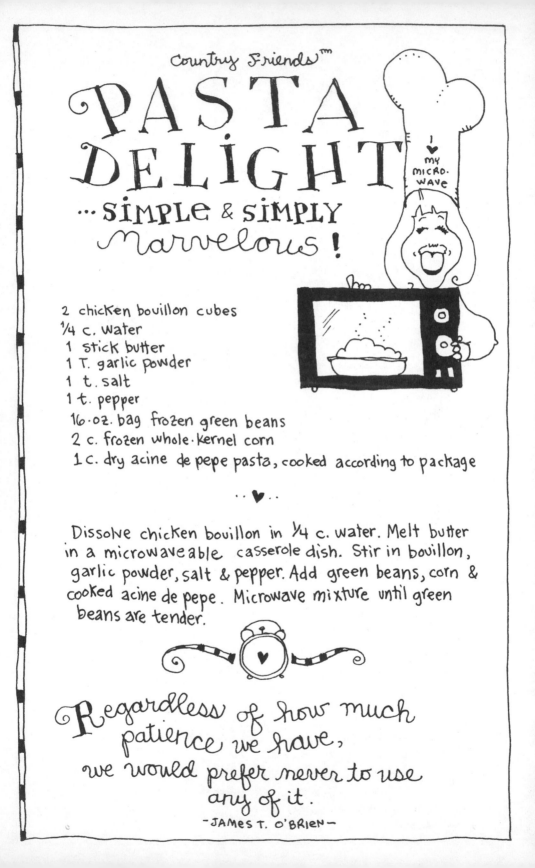

2 chicken bouillon cubes
¼ c. water
1 stick butter
1 T. garlic powder
1 t. salt
1 t. pepper
16-oz. bag frozen green beans
2 c. frozen whole-kernel corn
1 c. dry acine de pepe pasta, cooked according to package

·· ♥ ··

Dissolve chicken bouillon in ¼ c. water. Melt butter in a microwaveable casserole dish. Stir in bouillon, garlic powder, salt & pepper. Add green beans, corn & cooked acine de pepe. Microwave mixture until green beans are tender.

Regardless of how much patience we have, we would prefer never to use any of it.
— JAMES T. O'BRIEN —

Know the true value of time; snatch, seize, and **enjoy** every moment of it.
~Lord Chesterfield~

CAFE

Grab a
Country Friend™
&
get going...

CHAPTER 4:
Girls' Night Out

Form a bowling team!

ABSOLUTE NONSENSE

The key is to get out of the house ... play hooky from home ... graf your best buddies and go for the gusto! It's

GIRLS' NIGHT OUT

Go to a hard rock concert & scream uncontrollably!

Take a long walk to the closest ice cream shoppe!

Go to the mall & try on party or prom dresses!

* 32

Rent canoes ... and don't fall overboard!

TOMFOOLERY

69

THIS CERTIFIES THAT
Mary Elizabeth
IS AN
AUTHORIZED MEMBER OF THE CLUB.

START A

GOOD ♥ FRIENDS' GATHERING ♥ CLUB

YOU ARE INVITED!

Meet for dinner ··· dessert ··· an early riser breakfast ···
or
mid·morning munchies.

♥ CLUB RULES ♥

1. Meet once a month; say, every third Tuesday.
2. Pick a rendezvous spot ~ how about Large Marge's Muffin Shop?
3. choose a convenient time for friends to gather.
4. No excuses!

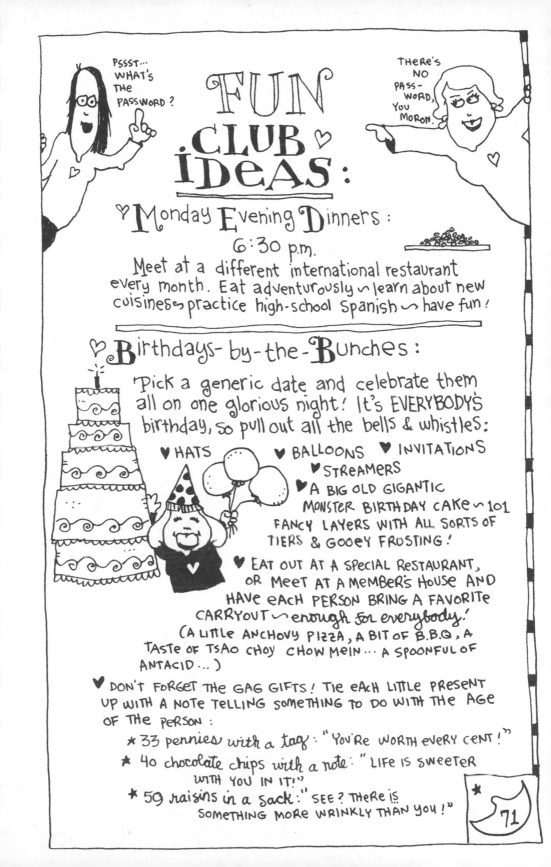

PSSST... WHAT'S THE PASSWORD?

THERE'S NO PASS-WORD, YOU MORON.

FUN CLUB IDEAS:

♥ Monday Evening Dinners:
6:30 p.m.

Meet at a different international restaurant every month. Eat adventurously ∼ learn about new cuisines ∼ practice high-school Spanish ∼ have fun!

♥ Birthdays-by-the-Bunches:

Pick a generic date and celebrate them all on one glorious night! It's EVERYBODY'S birthday, so pull out all the bells & whistles:

♥ HATS   ♥ BALLOONS   ♥ INVITATIONS
♥ STREAMERS
♥ A BIG OLD GIGANTIC MONSTER BIRTHDAY CAKE ∼ 101 FANCY LAYERS WITH ALL SORTS OF TIERS & GOOEY FROSTING!

♥ EAT OUT AT A SPECIAL RESTAURANT, OR MEET AT A MEMBER'S HOUSE AND HAVE EACH PERSON BRING A FAVORITE CARRYOUT ∼ enough for everybody! (A LITTLE ANCHOVY PIZZA, A BIT OF B.B.Q, A TASTE OF TSAO CHOY CHOW MEIN... A SPOONFUL OF ANTACID...)

♥ DON'T FORGET THE GAG GIFTS! TIE EACH LITTLE PRESENT UP WITH A NOTE TELLING SOMETHING TO DO WITH THE AGE OF THE PERSON:

* 33 pennies with a tag: "YOU'RE WORTH EVERY CENT!"
* 40 chocolate chips with a note: "LIFE IS SWEETER WITH YOU IN IT!"
* 59 raisins in a sack: "SEE? THERE IS SOMETHING MORE WRINKLY THAN YOU!"

★ 71

GAME

DIG OUT ALL THOSE OLD BOARD GAMES FOR AN EVENING OF GOOD, CLEAN F•U•N !

CHECKERS
TWISTER
SCRABBLE
CLUE
MONOPOLY
TIDDLY WINKS

Host a game night at your house. Set up card tables with different board games, and let guests choose their own game ... or everyone join in one big rambunctious round of Monopoly. Wheel, deal, eat, drink & pass go! Just have a good time!

I wanted to be the dog.

N·IGHT

SERVE EASY TREATS & ICY COLD POP IN CANS (don't forget the bendy straws!) and SWEETS TO EAT:

YUM·YUMS

A RICH and GOOEY TREAT!

40 CARAMELS
½ c. SWEETENED CONDENSED MILK
½ c. MARGARINE
LARGE MARSHMALLOWS
CRISPED RICE CEREAL

★

IN A HEAVY SAUCEPAN, MELT TOGETHER CARAMELS, CONDENSED MILK & MARGARINE OVER LOW HEAT. DIP LARGE MARSHMALLOWS IN MIXTURE ON TOOTHPICK OR BAMBOO SKEWER. ROLL IN CRISPED RICE CEREAL.

1ST PRIZE
2nd prize
3rd prize
GRACE LAND

GIVE OUT SILLY PRIZES TO EVERYONE, even the LOSERS!

★ white elephant gifts ~ visit your local thrift shop for ugly ceramic vases, souvenir ashtrays & paintings on velvet.

★ Big bundles of play money — buy it at the toy store, or be clever & make some with your photo on it! Be generous ~ give millions!

Have a Make-It-And-Take-It-Craft Night.

Every month, meet at a different friend's house & learn to make a craft for Christmas. By the time December rolls around, you'll have enough neat new gifts & decorations to go around! Keep the craft simple enough to complete in one night, then take 'em home & hide 'em for the holidays. Here are a couple of ideas to get you started:

FROSTY the SOAPMAN

* * * * * *

He's SILLY...
He's LUMPY...
BUT YOU'LL LOVE HIM

* * * * *

YOU NEED:
* 2 c. LAUNDRY SOAP (THE KIND FOR BABY CLOTHES)
* ¼ c. water
* toothpicks
* twigs
* buttons

* * * * * *

To make snow, pour LAUNDRY SOAP into a deep bowl. Add water & whip with an electric mixer until doughy. Scoop out doughy stuff with hands & shape into balls. Connect with toothpicks into snowman figures & decorate with twig arms & button eyes.

COUNTRY FRIENDS™ YULE LOGS

...A BEAUTIFUL GIFT!

YOU NEED:
* BIRCH LOGS (OR ANY LOGS) CUT INTO 18-20" LONG PIECES, ABOUT 8" DIAMETER
* RED-CHECKED RIBBON OR ANY HOLIDAY RIBBON YOU LIKE
* SPRIGS OF EVERGREEN, ROSEMARY & OTHER HERBS YOU HAVE ON HAND
* HOT GLUE GUN

*

TIE RIBBONS AROUND EACH END OF LOG & FASTEN SECURELY WITH A KNOT & DAB OF HOT-GLUE. TIE IN BOWS OR LEAVE RIBBONS LONG IF YOU WISH. BETWEEN THE RIBBONS ALONG THE TOP OF THE LOG, HOT-GLUE SPRIGS OF EVERGREEN & ROSEMARY IN A NICE ARRANGEMENT. GIVE LOG TO FRIENDS FOR FIREPLACE OR TABLE DECOR WITH INSTRUCTIONS TO BURN THE LOG ON CHRISTMAS EVE & AS THE SMOKE RISES TO SAY A PRAYER FOR THE COMING YEAR... a beautiful sentiment.

Look at it as an *extended* Girls' Night Out!
There's nothing like a road trip to break routine,
whether it's a day trip just down the highway or
a weekend-long jaunt 'cross the border :

an antiquers' treasure hunt at backroad shops & stops

a visit to the big city to ooh-and-aah at the Christmas lights

A garden tour of arboretums & conservatories, too

a pilgrimage to the state's best café, serving world-class apple pie à la mode

a shop-til-you-drop-athon at every factory outlet and road-side stand you see

culture shock: museum after museum after museum visit

a Girlfriends-only jaunt to the amusement park to ride the roller coaster

PILE IN!

77

KATE'S
TESTED-&-TRUE
RULES
FOR
SUCCESSFUL
DAY-
TRIPPERS

★ When traveling with old friends, be courteous: no pinching, no hitting, no pulling hair, no name-calling.

★ Don't offer to be the navigator unless you're prepared to be the official map-folder as well.

★ Be flexible as to trip music. Your tape of the Bavarian Yodeling Championships may not be everyone's favorite.

★ Don't chew tobacco, watermelon-scented bubblegum or garlic beef jerky in a crowded car.

★ Resist the temptation to spend your whole wad at the first rest-stop on pecan logs, indian drums & postcards of giant jackrabbits. You'll want to save some so you can buy travel-bingo cards at the next stop.

★ Go before you leave.

Follow the FUN

The whole point of a road-trip is to have a change of scenery. So get in the car and go... go for the totally **Unexpected:**

TAKE A FISHING TRIP WITH THE GIRLS. CAMP OUT & SLEEP UNDER THE STARS.

GO TO A BASEBALL GAME OR WRESTLING MATCH WITHOUT YOUR REGULAR MALE COMPANIONS.... GIRLS ONLY!

WHATSA MATTER, ARE YOU BLIND UMP??!

SPEND THE WEEKEND AT A DUDE RANCH OR ON A WORKING FARM ~ YIPPEE-KI-YO!

Enjoy the RIDE

* TAKE ALONG A BOOK ON TAPE – A MYSTERY IS FUN.

* TAKE FREQUENT STOPS TO STRETCH YOUR LEGS & SWITCH SEATS.

* GOSSIP, OR SOLVE ALL THE WORLD'S PROBLEMS ON THOSE LONG STRETCHES OF HIGHWAY.

* SING! WE LIKE OLD ELVIS TAPES ~ MOTOWN, TOO.

* AND, OF COURSE, EATS ARE A MUST FOR TRAVELLING SATISFACTION. TAKE ALONG A BAG OF THESE TO KEEP YOUR KATE QUIET:

PEACE & QUIET snack mix

...THE ONLY SOUND YOU'LL HEAR IS MUNCHING.

5 c. CRISPY CEREAL SQUARES (ANY COMBO-RICE, WHEAT, CORN)
1 c. ROUND TOASTED OAT CEREAL
½ c. PRETZEL STICKS
½ c. MIXED NUTS
½ c. BITE-SIZED CHEESE CRACKERS
1 STICK BUTTER OR MARGARINE
1 T. WORCESTERSHIRE SAUCE
1 T. TABASCO SAUCE
¼ t. GARLIC POWDER
¼ t. CELERY SALT

MIX CEREALS, PRETZELS, NUTS & CRACKERS IN A SHALLOW ROASTING PAN. MELT BUTTER OR MARGARINE IN SAUCEPAN. STIR IN WORCESTERSHIRE, TABASCO & SPICES. POUR OVER CEREAL MIXTURE IN ROASTING PAN ~ STIR GENTLY TO COAT. BAKE AT 350° FOR 30 MINUTES, STIRRING EVERY 10 MINUTES.

79

You are invited
to a

No~ Good~ Reason SHOWER

US!

honoring ....
date ....
time ....
place ....
given by ....
please bring a gift-wrapped
....
RSVP by .... phone ....

↳ COPY OUR INVITATION OR MAKE YOUR OWN

Really desperate
for a good reason to
get together?

Bathroom towels getting pretty
ratty after 16 years of
housekeeping?

Follow Kate's fine example:
*throw yourself
a
Shower!*

That's right. You don't need to wait for a
legitimate engagement or upcoming birth to
have a party. Just come up with a guest list
of friends who haven't been on the receiving
end of a shower invitation lately and honor
them with a real, honest-to-goodness

big Shower of gifts & good wishes.

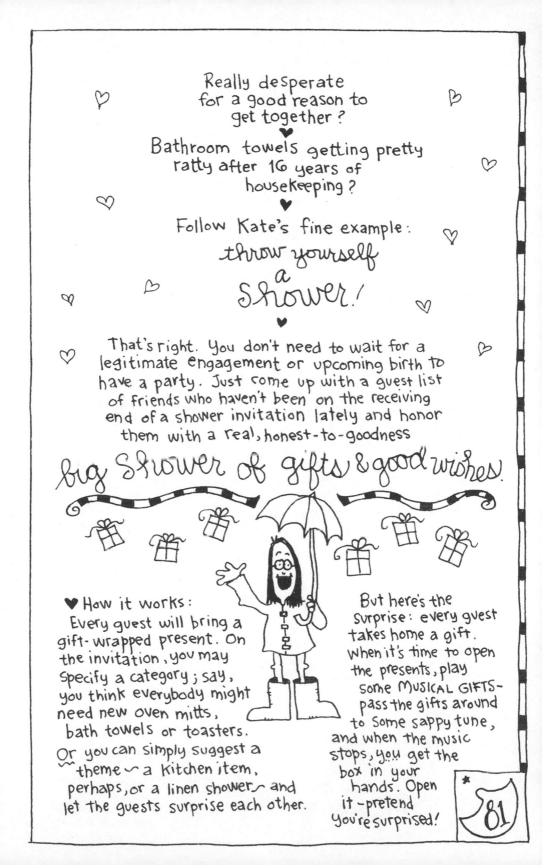

♥ How it works:
Every guest will bring a
gift-wrapped present. On
the invitation, you may
specify a category; say,
you think everybody might
need new oven mitts,
bath towels or toasters.
Or you can simply suggest a
theme ~ a kitchen item,
perhaps, or a linen shower ~ and
let the guests surprise each other.

But here's the
surprise: every guest
takes home a gift.
When it's time to open
the presents, play
some MUSICAL GIFTS-
pass the gifts around
to some sappy tune,
and when the music
stops, you get the
box in your
hands. Open
it - pretend
you're surprised!

81

No · Good · Reason · Shower Refreshments

♥

What do you expect?
♥ Punch ♥ Cake
Served on your best crystal plates,
of course!
~ and ~

Party mints

♥ a nice touch:
pink cupcakes
with plastic
bridal folks
on top

20·OZ. PKG. WHITE ALMOND BARK
6 PEPPERMINT STICKS OR CANDY CANES,
CRUSHED
♥
Break almond bark into pieces. Place 3 to 4
pieces in a microwave-safe glass bowl. Watch
carefully ~ microwave until soft enough to stir,
about 2 to 3 minutes. Stir in part of crushed
peppermint candy. Thinly spread mixture onto
a wax-paper-lined cookie sheet. Freeze 5 to 10
minutes. When firm, break into pieces. Repeat
with remaining bark & candy.

♥ go
HEAVY
with the
crêpe paper
decorations &
paper bells

♥ A good·time
no·good·reason·
Shower game:
provide plain
white paper
plates,
chartreuse tulle &
a stapler to
each guest to
see who can
make the best/
worst bridesmaid
bonnet in 3
minutes.

♥ For added fun,
ask your guests to come
wearing bridesmaids' dresses.
guess whose came from
the local thrift shops,
and who still had several
old ones hanging
in her closet.

CIRCA 1970 →

♥ Play sentimental background
music ~ Mantovani,
Burt Bacharach wedding tunes.

Friends are a second existence.

— BALTASAR GRACIAN —

OTHER FUN STUFF to do on GIRLS' NIGHT OUT:

Movie Madness: go see two movies in a row!

Go out for Dessert & Coffee.

Break a Leg: see a musical or play. If Broadway is too far away, check out a tempting high school or college performance.

PLAY BILL

admit 1

admit 1

Volunteer ~

A GREAT WAY TO SPEND QUALITY TIME WITH YOUR FRIENDS & DO A GOOD DEED AS WELL

Read at a library or record books on tape for the sight-impaired.

Tutors are a blessing to those who need extra help.

Visit a nursing home once a month with friends... check to see if pets are welcome, too.

Volunteer at your local animal shelter.

Adopt a park or part of your neighborhood to clean-up with friends.

TRASH

please don't litter

Gardening by Committee

No time for gardening? Garden by group! Find a place for a flower or veggie patch, and with a bunch of friends, plan, prepare & Enjoy the pleasures of the garden.

Everyone should be prepared to work a little every few days to keep your plot weeded & watered ~ plus, schedule an early evening meeting in the garden every week for fellowship & fertilization, cultivation & companionship! Share the harvest... and the fun. (THIS IS A WONDERFUL PROJECT TO START AT A SENIOR CITIZEN RESIDENCE ~ ASK AT A LOCAL HOME FOR A LITTLE GARDEN SPOT TO SHARE WITH RESIDENTS.)

85

Holly's Big Night Out with the girls I•D•E•A:

1. Find the most luxurious local hotel in your town.
2. Reserve a room with 2 king-size beds.
3. Pick up your best 3 non-snoring girlfriends.
4. Check into the hotel at 5 p.m. with your entourage.
5. Put on your jammies and order room service.
6. Splurge on an in-room movie ~ hopefully, a classic tear-jerker.
7. Lay around on the bed all evening. Only move to run to the ice machine.
8. Sleep late the next morning, then eat big brunch before going home, all refreshed & pampered.

Make Work-Outs a Team Effort

You're more likely to keep at it if you exercise with a friend.

* Join an *aerobics class*.
* Find a good *walking partner*.
* Form a *softball team*.

Thanks – but I prefer non-sweating activities.

CHAPTER 5: Pure Pleasures

Time for a little something.
— Winnie the pooh —

It's a dirty job
but the
Country Friends™
show you
how to
do it
right...

DOG
Food

RISE and SHINE BIG BREAKFAST

Forget fat! No counting calories today!
Treat your family to a big farm-style breakfast:

Buttermilk pancakes

Hash Browns

Warm Biscuits

Butter

Bacon

Milk

Fresh Fruit

CHEESY EGG SCRAMBLE

THEY'LL SCRAMBLE OUT OF BED FOR THESE...

2 T. ONION, CHOPPED
1 T. OIL
5 EGGS
⅓ C. MILK
⅛ t. PEPPER
¼ t. SALT
⅓ c. CHEESE, GRATED
BACON, COOKED & CRUMBLED

SAUTÉ ONION & OIL IN BIG SKILLET. ADD EGGS, MILK, PEPPER & SALT ~ MIX TOGETHER AND COOK OVER MEDIUM HEAT. ADD CHEESE. TURN GENTLY AS MIXTURE COOKS. JUST BEFORE SERVING, SPRINKLE WITH BACON.

(6 SERVINGS)

MOMMY'S APPLES & SAUSAGE

SOOOOO GOOD!

2 LBS. SAUSAGE LINKS
⅓ C. WATER
¼ C. BROWN SUGAR
2 LG. TART APPLES, SLICED
1 LG. ONION, CHOPPED

BROWN SAUSAGES IN BIG SKILLET; DRAIN ON PAPER TOWELS. ADD OTHER INGREDIENTS TO SAME PAN. COOK 8 TO 10 MINUTES 'TIL TENDER, THEN STIR SAUSAGES INTO MIXTURE. COOK ADDITIONAL 8 TO 10 MINUTES.

(6 SERVINGS)

THAT WAS GREAT. GOOD NIGHT NOW.

Pure Pleasures: The Big Breakfast

STUFFeD FReNCH ToASTieS

↪ THE ONLY THING TO GET HOLLY TO THE TABLE WITHOUT HER MAKE-UP ON. .....

4 EGGS, BEATEN
½ C. MILK
¼ C. BROWN SUGAR
½ t. CINNAMON
1 t. VANILLA
.....

FRENCH BREAD, THICK-SLICED

FRESH FRUIT- SLICED

POWDERED SUGAR

COMBINE EGGS & MILK IN MIXING BOWL. ADD IN SUGAR & CINNAMON — WHISK WELL. STIR IN VANILLA.

TAKE SLICE OF BREAD— MAKE SLIT IN CENTER. STUFF SLIT WITH FRUIT. DIP BREAD INTO BATTER. DEEP-FRY 'TIL GOLDEN BROWN. SPRINKLE WITH POWDERED SUGAR BEFORE SERVING.

OtHeR Breakfast GooDieS:

* dress up a naked grapefruit half with a drizzle of honey & a dash of cinnamon & a quick sit under the broiler for 2 minutes!

* frozen fruit salads in muffin tins are delicious breakfast treats served alongside waffles.

* puree ripe fruit & add softened butter & powdered sugar to it to make delightful homemade fruit butters for pancakes & muffins!

Cultivate the habit of early rising. ...It is unwise to keep the head long on a level with the feet. —THOREAU

...A fine start to someone's special day!

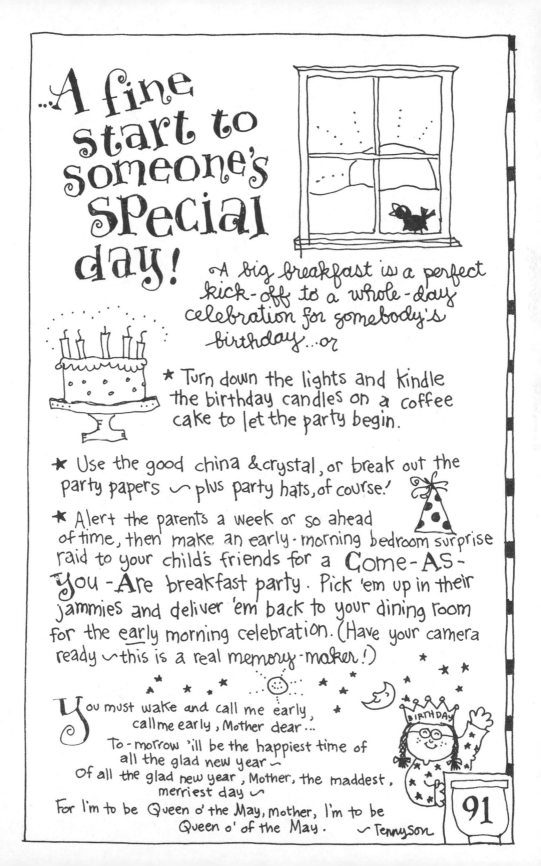

A big breakfast is a perfect kick-off to a whole-day celebration for somebody's birthday...or

★ Turn down the lights and kindle the birthday candles on a coffee cake to let the party begin.

★ Use the good china & crystal, or break out the party papers ⌣ plus party hats, of course!

★ Alert the parents a week or so ahead of time, then make an early-morning bedroom surprise raid to your child's friends for a Come-As-You-Are breakfast party. Pick 'em up in their jammies and deliver 'em back to your dining room for the early morning celebration. (Have your camera ready ⌣ this is a real memory-maker!)

You must wake and call me early,
    call me early, Mother dear...
To-morrow 'ill be the happiest time of
    all the glad new year ⌣
Of all the glad new year, Mother, the maddest,
    merriest day ⌣
For I'm to be Queen o' the May, Mother, I'm to be
        Queen o' of the May.   ⌣ Tennyson

91

Summer's

Oh, sweet summer! Bare feet in cool green grass... the refreshing run through the sprinkler on a hot July afternoon... the twinkle of fireflies in the warm evening sky... for pure pleasure, there's nothing like the good old summertime.

Take the vow that this summer, you'll take full advantage of the season's little luxuries — no whining about the heat (well, ok, a little bit), no eating canned fruits & vegetables, no opportunity for summer fun passed by!

Repeat after us:

* I will fly a kite this summer with my kids.

* I will run around like a maniac in a warm rain shower, minus shoes & rainhat.

pleasures

* I will sit on a porch swing with an old friend.
* I will take a walk after dark and listen to the crickets.
* I will forget what my thighs look like and don a swim suit for fun in the pool!
* I will write my name against the night sky with a sparkler.
* I will get out to the Farmer's Market before all the fresh raspberries are gone.
* I will lay in the hammock with a trashy novel, iced tea & no phone.
* I will enjoy the pleasures of summer.

I will, I will, I will!

Summer's Pleasures

HOST A GO BANANAS

Ice Cream Social

...A PERFECT WAY TO
CELEBRATE THE END OF THE SCHOOL YEAR and THE
BEGINNING OF SUMMER! LET YOUR KIDS TAKE THE LEAD
IN PLANNING THIS PARTY ~ FROM INVITING THEIR FRIENDS,
TEACHERS, FAMILY & NEIGHBORS TO PICKING OUT THE ICE
CREAM TOPPINGS, THIS CELEBRATION IS THEIRS... KIDS, SUMMER
& ICE CREAM... WHAT'S A MORE NATURAL COMBINATION?

HAND·DELIVER

invitations

AROUND THE
NEIGHBORHOOD:

FILL A SUGAR CONE WITH
COLORFUL SHREDDED TISSUE
(AVAILABLE AT PARTY STORES &
GIFT WRAP SECTIONS OF SHOPS)~
REALLY STUFF IT FULL AND LET
THE TISSUE POP OUT THE TOP OF THE
CONE! DROP IT IN A CLEAR PLASTIC
BAG WITH A COPY OF PARTY INVITATION
PARTICULARS ~ date, time, place ~ AND
TIE SHUT WITH CURLING RIBBON.

come to an
Ice Cream Social
Saturday June 3
molly's Backyard

SET OUT A VARIETY OF YUMMY TOPPINGS & ICE CREAMS and LET GUESTS MAKE THEIR OWN

Banana Splits!

SPRINKLES

BERRIES

BUTTER-SCOTCH

CHERRIES

CHOCOLATE CHIPS

WHIPPED CREAM

THE ULTIMATE FUDGE SAUCE

2 oz. unsweetened chocolate
3/4 c. sugar
1/4 t. salt
1/2 c. light corn syrup
1/2 c. milk
2 T. butter
1 T. vanilla

Combine first 5 ingredients in a saucepan, cook for 20 minutes over low heat ~ stir often. Add butter. Cool slightly, then add vanilla.

Just right over ice cream!

♥ Ask at your local ice cream shop if you can buy some plastic banana split dishes... ice cream just tastes better out of them!

Homemade 'Nilla Ice Cream

6 eggs
1 QT. MILK
2 c. SUGAR
1/2 t. SALT
1 QT. HEAVY CREAM
5 t. VANILLA EXTRACT

Combine eggs & milk in saucepan. Using a whisk, beat 'til well-blended. Add sugar & salt. Cook on low heat 'til it begins to thicken. Put saucepan in cold water ~ let cool. Mix cream & vanilla well ~ blend into cooled egg mixture. Chill at least 1 hour. Pour into ice cream maker, following manufacturer's directions and...

start cranking!

95

A Sunny Day PiE in the sky Party

Host a pie party! Set up a long table under the shade trees, toss on a cheerful tablecloth and sit a spell with friends & neighbors. Have each guest bring a favorite pie ~ you provide the ice-cold milk!

Hey!! Me!! Me!

I'll do it!

choose Me!

Yo!!

Me!

K

IT'S A NATURAL... A Pie·Eater's contest!

SLICE A JUICY BLUEBERRY PIE INTO 6 PIECES AND ASK FOR VOLUNTEERS FOR A NO-HANDS-PIE-EATING CONTEST. TIE ON SOME BIBS AND KEEP YOUR CAMERA READY FOR HILARIOUS SHOTS.

USE DISPOSABLE ALUMINUM PIE PLATES FOR GUESTS TO SERVE THEMSELVES.

Bring it on

our pie party recipes

ASK YOUR GUESTS TO BRING THE RECIPE ALONG WITH THEIR PIE ~ SOMEONE IS SURE TO ASK FOR IT! MAKE COPIES AVAILABLE AT THE PARTY ~ OR ASSEMBLE THE RECIPES INTO A CASUAL THANK YOU "COOKBOOK" (PHOTOCOPIES TIED TOGETHER WITH RED RIBBONS) AND MAIL THEM, ALONG WITH CONTEST PHOTOS, AFTER THE PARTY ~ TO EACH GUEST.

97

NO BLACKBIRD PIE, PLEASE.

Ode to Pie

by Kate

ahem.

Pies are good
Pies are fine
'specially chocolate
and old key lime
but to make me hoppy
put more stuff
     on toppy.

Like:

a slice of
Cheddar cheese

whipped cream

cinnamon
sugar

chocolate
syrup

fresh fruit

chocolate shavings

freshly grated
coconut

copy & color
if you
wish→

♥ absolute ♥
very
BEST
PIE of
♥ S·H·O·W ♥

BLUE· RIBBON PIES all around

Every pie is a winner at
your party! Have blue
ribbons ready or copy ours
(above) and hot·glue the
medallion to a blue gingham
ribbon, then simply fill·in·the
blank with the pie name, and
lay it beside the treat on the
table.

*...great eats
and great fun!*

Kate's Chocolate Chip Piggy Pie

... THREE GUESSES AS TO WHY IT'S CALLED THAT!

2 eggs
½ c. flour
½ c. white sugar
½ c. brown sugar
1 c. butter, melted & cooled
1 c. semi-sweet chocolate chips
1 c. chopped walnuts
1 unbaked 9" pie shell

In a mixing bowl, beat eggs until foamy. Add flour & sugars ~ beat until blended. Blend in butter. Stir in chips & nuts. Pour into pie shell. Bake at 375° for 40 minutes. Serve warm with vanilla ice cream.

My Oh My Peach Pie

WE dECLARE! THE BEST PEACH PIE I EVER DID EAT!

4 c. peaches, quartered & peeled
½ c. sugar
½ t. nutmeg
dash salt
1 egg
2 T. cream

½ c. flour
¼ c. brown sugar
2 T. butter
9" unbaked pie shell

ARRANGE PEACHES IN PIE SHELL ~ SPRINKLE WITH SUGAR, NUTMEG & SALT. BEAT EGG & CREAM ~ POUR OVER PEACHES. MIX FLOUR, BROWN SUGAR & BUTTER 'TIL CRUMBLY, THEN SPRINKLE OVER PIE. BAKE AT 425° FOR 35 to 45 MINUTES.

My oh My!

99

SNAPPY APPLE KATE

We know, we know, it's really Apple Brown Betty but it's our book and we can call it whatever we want!

IT'S PRACTICALLY A HEALTH FOOD - THE APPLES, YOU KNOW.

⅓ c. water
⅓ c. bourbon or apple juice
⅓ c. golden raisins
1 t. vanilla extract

2½ lbs. tart apples, peeled & cut into chunks
⅓ c. sugar
2 c. fresh whole grain breadcrumbs
6 T. butter, melted
¼ c. brown sugar, packed
½ t. cinnamon

...

Bring water & bourbon to boil in saucepan. Add raisins & vanilla ~ remove from heat, cover, let stand 'til cool. Transfer raisins & liquid to big bowl. Add apples & sugar ~ toss well. Mix breadcrumbs, butter, brown sugar & cinnamon. Spoon half of apples into 8" glass baking dish. Top with half of breadcrumbs. Repeat layering with remaining apples & crumbs. Bake at 375° for 50-60 minutes.

Personal Favorites

There is no disputing about tastes.

— Latin proverb

Mary Elizabeth's Best
SMASHED TATERS

Not technically
a dessert but they
qualify as a
pure pleasure,
that's for sure!

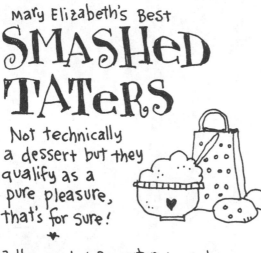

3 lbs. peeled & quartered potatoes
1 c. grated parmesan cheese
½ c. butter
3 green onions, sliced
1 clove garlic, minced
½ c. whipping cream
...

Cook taters in a pan of boiling
water 'til very tender—about
25 minutes. Drain; return to
pan. Beat with electric mixer.

In another bowl, combine
cheese, butter, onions & garlic.
Beat with mixer 'til mixture
is almost smooth.

Add cheese mixture to potatoes
& cream. Beat with electric
mixer until very creamy.
Season with salt & pepper to
taste.

mmmmarvelous!

HOLLY'S WHITE CHOCOLATE THRILLS

These set our
little ♥s
to pitter-
pattering!

1¼ lb. almond bark
1½ c. miniature
    marshmallows
1½ c. peanut butter
    cereal
1½ c. crisp rice cereal
1½ c. mixed nuts
½ c. mini chocolate
    chips
...

In a casserole dish,
melt almond bark in
200° oven for 25
minutes; stir occasionally.
Place marshmallows,
cereal, nuts & chocolate
chips in bowl. Pour
melted bark over mixture,
stirring to coat. Drop
by spoonfuls onto
waxed paper ~ allow to
set.

101

ASK THE EXPERT: KATE ANSWERS YOUR CHOCOLATE INQUIRIES

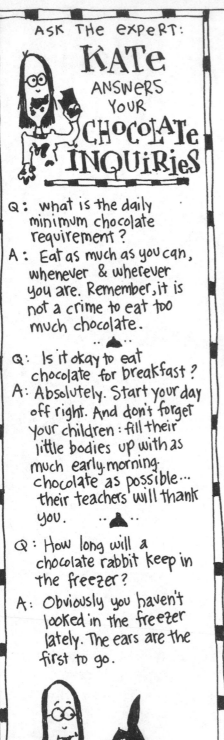

Q: What is the daily minimum chocolate requirement?

A: Eat as much as you can, whenever & wherever you are. Remember, it is not a crime to eat too much chocolate.

Q: Is it okay to eat chocolate for breakfast?

A: Absolutely. Start your day off right. And don't forget your children: fill their little bodies up with as much early-morning chocolate as possible... their teachers will thank you.

Q: How long will a chocolate rabbit keep in the freezer?

A: Obviously you haven't looked in the freezer lately. The ears are the first to go.

The ULTIMATE CHOCOLATE experience

Good morning. Your assignment, should you decide to accept it, is admittedly a dangerous one. It may result in cavities, tummy-ache or a decided turning-away from chocolate. However, the rewards of the mission can be enormous (as can your possible weight gain)— Please weigh the options carefully and proceed with our good wishes if you so decide.

May the force be with you.

Chocolate 'Round the Clock

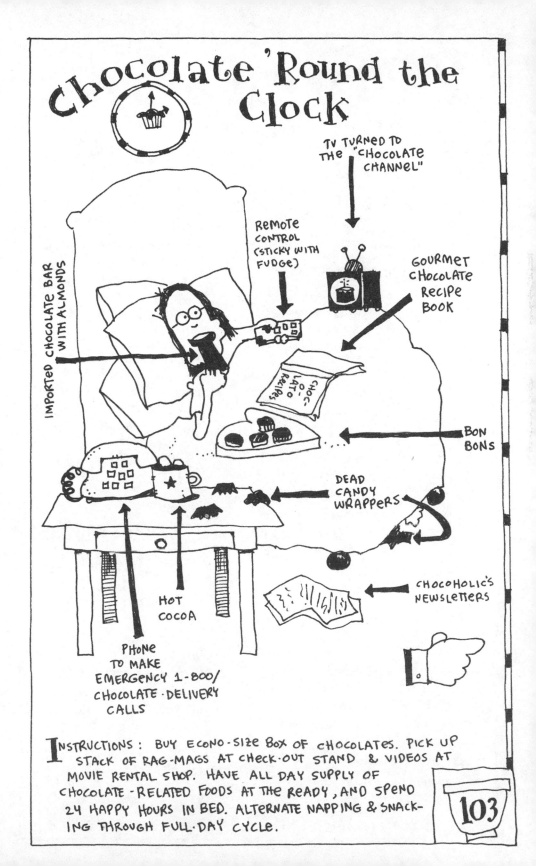

TV TURNED TO THE "CHOCOLATE CHANNEL"

REMOTE CONTROL (STICKY WITH FUDGE)

GOURMET CHOCOLATE RECIPE BOOK

IMPORTED CHOCOLATE BAR WITH ALMONDS

CHOC-O-LATO RECIPES

BON BONS

DEAD CANDY WRAPPERS

CHOCOHOLIC'S NEWSLETTERS

HOT COCOA

PHONE TO MAKE EMERGENCY 1-800/ CHOCOLATE·DELIVERY CALLS

INSTRUCTIONS : BUY ECONO·SIZE BOX OF CHOCOLATES. PICK UP STACK OF RAG·MAGS AT CHECK·OUT STAND & VIDEOS AT MOVIE RENTAL SHOP. HAVE ALL DAY SUPPLY OF CHOCOLATE·RELATED FOODS AT THE READY, AND SPEND 24 HAPPY HOURS IN BED. ALTERNATE NAPPING & SNACKING THROUGH FULL·DAY CYCLE.

103

24 hours of

7 a.m.
Good Morning Cocoa

⅓ c. COCOA
⅓ c. SUGAR
3½ c. MILK
½ c. WATER
½ t. VANILLA
pinch of salt

MIX COCOA, SUGAR & SALT IN PAN. ADD WATER & BRING TO BOIL FOR 1 MINUTE. STIR IN MILK — HEAT WELL BUT DO NOT BOIL. ADD VANILLA & STIR WELL.

8 a.m.
Coco-Waffles

2 EGGS, WELL-BEATEN
¾ c. CREAM
1¼ c. CAKE FLOUR
½ t. SALT
3 t. BAKING POWDER
6 T. COCOA
½ c. SUGAR
¼ c. BUTTER, MELTED
2 EGG WHITES, STIFFLY BEATEN
¼ t. VANILLA

BLEND WHOLE EGGS & CREAM. SIFT TOGETHER ALL DRY INGREDIENTS — STIR INTO EGG MIXTURE. ADD BUTTER & VANILLA TO MIXTURE — MIX WELL. FOLD IN EGG WHITES. BAKE IN WAFFLE IRON. TOP WITH ICE CREAM (CHOCOLATE, OF COURSE).

1 P.M.
Chocolate Fruit Dip

(CAUTION: THIS CONTAINS FRUIT, WHICH IS GOOD FOR YOU)

8 OZ. SEMI SWEET CHOCOLATE
1 C. SHREDDED COCONUT
ASST. FROZEN FRUITS - BANANAS & GRAPES & CUT-UP FRESH APPLES

MELT CHOCOLATE IN SMALL PAN. USE BAMBOO SKEWER TO PIERCE FRUIT INTO "KABOBS" THEN ROLL FRUIT IN MELTED CHOCOLATE. ROLL IN SHREDDED COCONUT. FREEZE ON WAXED PAPER OR EAT NOW!

3 P.M.
Chocolate Lemonade

...A MID-AFTERNOON REFRESHER!

USING A 12-OZ. CAN OF FROZEN LEMONADE CONCENTRATE, PREPARE A PITCHER-FULL ACCORDING TO PACKAGE DIRECTIONS. ADD ¼ c. OF CHOCOLATE SYRUP TO THE PITCHER — MIX WELL. DRINK OVER ICE.

4 - 6 P.M.: more candy.

9 - 12 P.M.: ASSORTED CANDY.

CHOCO BAR

Chocolate

7 P.M.
HOT FUDGE PUDDING CAKE

I've never been happier in my life.

...TIME TO GET SERIOUS ABOUT THIS CHOCOLATE THING NOW!

1 c. FLOUR	2 T. OIL
3/4 c. SUGAR	1 t. VANILLA
2 T. COCOA	1 c. CHOPPED NUTS
2 t. BAKING POWDER	1/4 c. COCOA
1/4 t. SALT	1 c. BROWN SUGAR
1/2 c. MILK	1·3/4 c. VERY HOT WATER

COMBINE FLOUR, SUGAR, COCOA, BAKING POWDER & SALT. BLEND IN MILK, OIL & VANILLA 'TIL SMOOTH. SPREAD INTO 9" SQUARE PAN. SPRINKLE WITH BROWN SUGAR & COCOA; POUR HOT WATER OVER BATTER — DO NOT STIR! BAKE 40 MINUTES AT 350°. SERVE WITH ICE CREAM.

9 P.M.
Peanut Butter Sandwich
with Chocolate Chips

SPREAD WHITE BREAD WITH PEANUT BUTTER. SPRINKLE WITH CHOCOLATE CHIPS & TOP WITH ADDITIONAL SLICE OF BREAD.

(NOTE: Peanut Butter is high in fat. Please don't over-do it.)

10 P.M.
CHOCOLATE SHAKE & SHOUT

COMBINE 1 c. COLD MILK & 1/4 c. CHOCOLATE SYRUP. ADD 1 PT. VANILLA ICE CREAM. BLEND. SPRINKLE TOP WITH CINNAMON.

10 P.M. – 7 A.M.
REPEAT Recipes
AS NECESSARY.

"Nine out of ten people like chocolate. The tenth person always lies."

— JOHN G. TULLIUS

105

BUT...

If you just **can't** have 'em,
try one of these little treats as a

consolation prize. ♥

A CUP OF COCOA WITH MARSHMALLOWS

AN AFTERNOON NAP

RE-RUNS OF OLD TV SHOWS

A LONG HOT SOAK IN A BUBBLY BATH

A DIP OF FROZEN YOGURT

NEW RED TOE-NAIL POLISH

A LENGTHY LONG-DISTANCE CHAT WITH AUNT EDNA

A PAGE-TURNING PAPERBACK

FRESH BERRIES WITH MILK

Life itself is the proper binge.

~ JULIA CHILD ~

FORGET IT! GIVE ME MY COOKIE DOUGH!

COUNTRY FRIENDS™

Pure Pleasures

Homemade Vegetable Soup on a cold day...

Hot bread right out of the oven with honey butter...

A fresh strawberry eaten out in the garden...

A long cool drink of water after a walk...

Grandma's pumpkin pie recipe.

Happiness is a way station between too little & too much.

—CHANNING POLLOCK—

BAD THINGS we Like to Eat that we should have OUTGROWN by now:

FROOT Twisties — Those fruit-flavored sugar-laden cereals sold by singing birds & dancing bears

CANDY NECKLACES made of edible "beads" & wax halloween teeth

(OH! And those little wax bottles filled with sweet syrupy stuff!)

COTTON CANDY

LICORICE WHIPS

POPCORN DRENCHED IN HOT BUTTER

We Love 'Em!

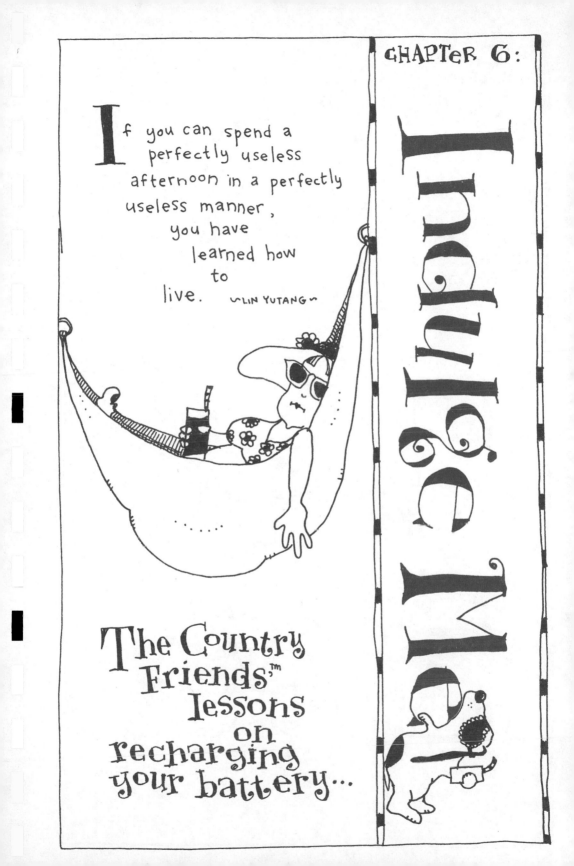

CHAPTER 6:

Indulge Me

I f you can spend a perfectly useless afternoon in a perfectly useless manner, you have learned how to live. ~LIN YUTANG~

The Country Friends™ lessons on recharging your battery...

Handy Things to have in your Hiding Place:

a flashlight

a journal & pen

headphones & cassette/CD player with soothing music

inspirational reading or poetry

3 months of canned food & bottled water in case you decide not to go back home for a while

The Country Friends™ on Running Away from Home

"When I can't take it anymore, I just hide in the laundry room. Nobody in the family ever goes in there but me, and if they did dare to enter, I'd just duck behind the mountain of unfolded stuff."
— Mary Elizabeth

"Play Hide & Go Seek. Let the kids hide, then just forget to go look for 'em for an hour or so."
— Holly

"I go to the movies and always feel better when I go home."
— Vickie

Got a lock on the BATHROOM DOOR?

Then You Have A

Home SPA

Kick off your shoes, hide the phone under a pillow and come on in ...

(SHUT THE DOOR BEHIND YOU & LOCK IT.)

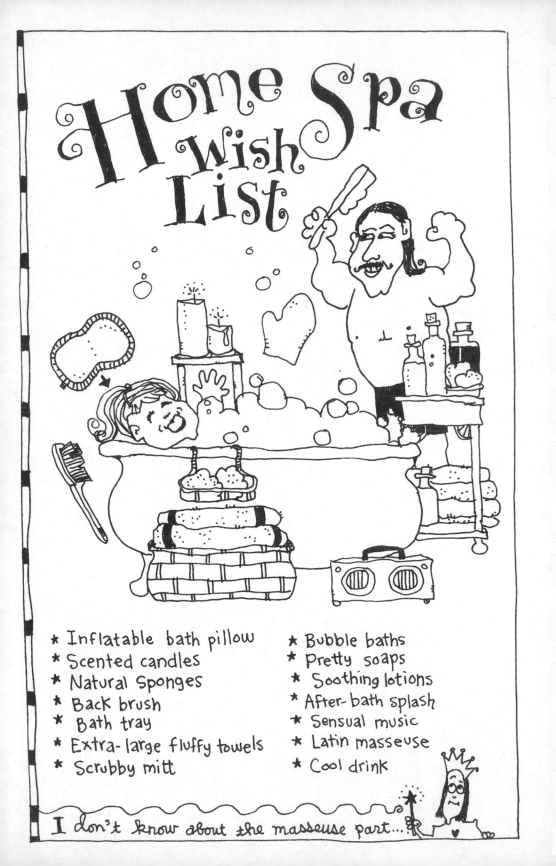

Home Spa Wish List

* Inflatable bath pillow
* Scented candles
* Natural Sponges
* Back brush
* Bath tray
* Extra-large fluffy towels
* Scrubby mitt

* Bubble baths
* Pretty soaps
* Soothing lotions
* After-bath splash
* Sensual music
* Latin masseuse
* Cool drink

I don't know about the masseuse part...

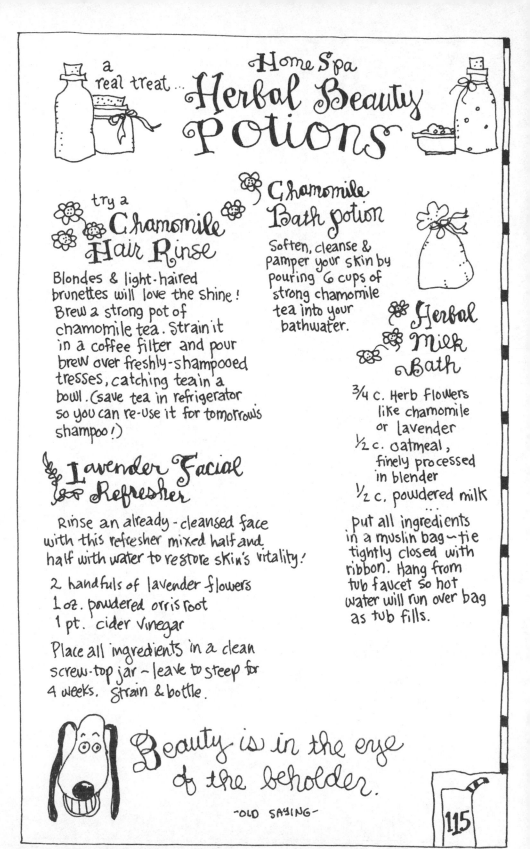

a real treat...

Home Spa
Herbal Beauty Potions

try a Chamomile Hair Rinse

Blondes & light-haired brunettes will love the shine! Brew a strong pot of chamomile tea. Strain it in a coffee filter and pour brew over freshly-shampooed tresses, catching tea in a bowl. (save tea in refrigerator so you can re-use it for tomorrow's shampoo!)

Lavender Facial Refresher

Rinse an already-cleansed face with this refresher mixed half and half with water to restore skin's vitality!

2 handfuls of lavender flowers
1 oz. powdered orris root
1 pt. cider vinegar

Place all ingredients in a clean screw-top jar ~ leave to steep for 4 weeks. Strain & bottle.

Chamomile Bath potion

Soften, cleanse & pamper your skin by pouring 6 cups of strong chamomile tea into your bathwater.

Herbal Milk Bath

3/4 c. Herb flowers like chamomile or lavender
1/2 c. oatmeal, finely processed in blender
1/2 c. powdered milk

...

put all ingredients in a muslin bag ~ tie tightly closed with ribbon. Hang from tub faucet so hot water will run over bag as tub fills.

Beauty is in the eye of the beholder.

-OLD SAYING-

115

AromA therapy

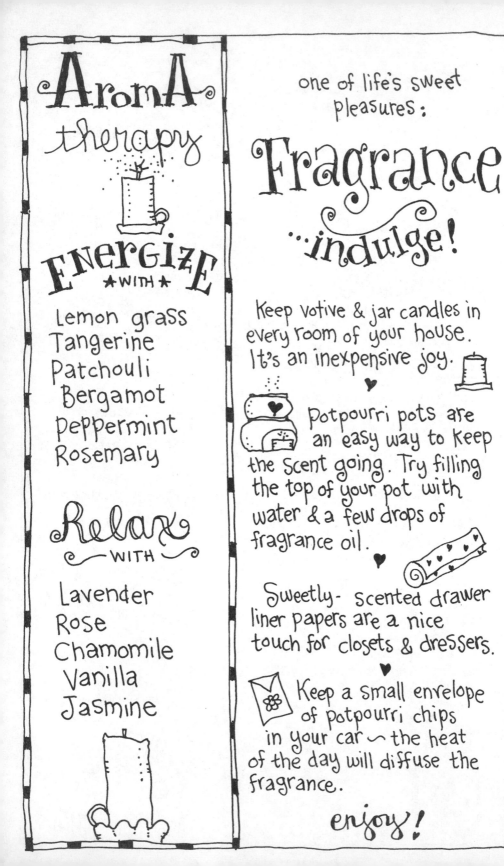

ENERGIZE ★ WITH ★

Lemon grass
Tangerine
Patchouli
Bergamot
Peppermint
Rosemary

Relax ～ WITH

Lavender
Rose
Chamomile
Vanilla
Jasmine

---

one of life's sweet pleasures:

Fragrance ...indulge!

Keep votive & jar candles in every room of your house. It's an inexpensive joy.

♥

Potpourri pots are an easy way to keep the scent going. Try filling the top of your pot with water & a few drops of fragrance oil.

♥

Sweetly-scented drawer liner papers are a nice touch for closets & dressers.

♥

Keep a small envelope of potpourri chips in your car ～ the heat of the day will diffuse the fragrance.

enjoy!

Vickie's FRAGRANT

Sweet Dreams infusion

...add herbal-infused water to the final rinse when laundering sheets, pillow cases and pajamas.

To make infusion: 4 c. boiling water
4 T. fresh herbs, leaves & flowers

Pour boiling water over herbs. Steep for 30 minutes. Strain and add to rinse water.

nice aromatic herbs to try: lavender, lemon balm, rose geranium, rosemary.

ROSEMARY   BASIL   MINT

Ooooo·La·La!

keep a bottle of your favorite fragrance in the refrigerator this summer ~ a little splash of icy perfume will give you a **Lift!**

Meditate.

(or pretend to)

All that's needed is a quiet spot and you.

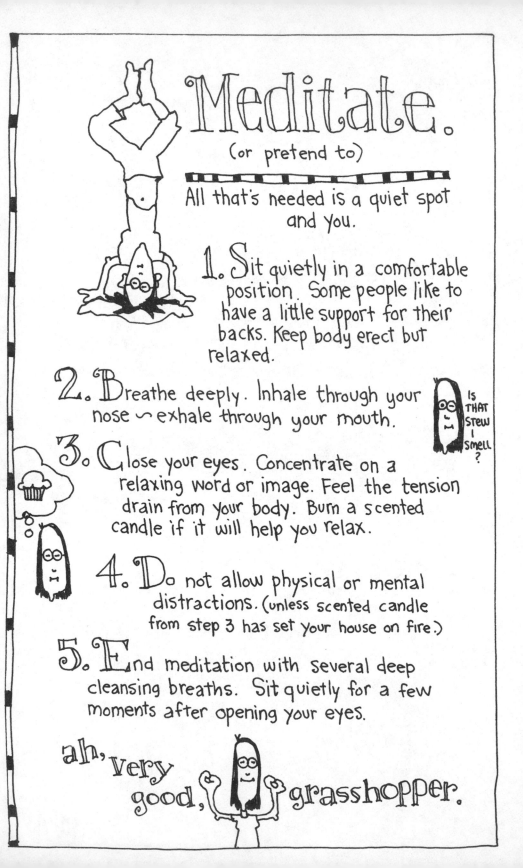

1. Sit quietly in a comfortable position. Some people like to have a little support for their backs. Keep body erect but relaxed.

2. Breathe deeply. Inhale through your nose ~ exhale through your mouth.

Is THAT STEW I SMELL ?

3. Close your eyes. Concentrate on a relaxing word or image. Feel the tension drain from your body. Burn a scented candle if it will help you relax.

4. Do not allow physical or mental distractions. (unless scented candle from step 3 has set your house on fire.)

5. End meditation with several deep cleansing breaths. Sit quietly for a few moments after opening your eyes.

ah, very good, grasshopper.

Relax.
(or try to)

Daydream.

Catnap.

Rock.

Swing.

Fingerpaint.

Read.

Float.

Quilt.

Vegetate.

Write.

Birdwatch.

Be Quiet.

God is the friend of silence. Trees, flowers, grass grow in silence. See the stars, moon and sun, how they move in silence.

~Mother Teresa~

119

yourself!

Drink Water!

Stretch Well!

Use the Stairs!

Breathe!

Limit Caffeine & Alcohol!

Play Lively Music!

121

EnergizE!
☆ EAT energy-BOOSTER food ☆

low-fat cheese

low-fat YOGURT

FRUITS

VEGETABLES

SKIM MILK

LOW-FAT PROTEIN SUCH AS BROILED CHICKEN, TURKEY, FISH OR DRIED BEANS

COMPLEX CARBOHYDRATES LIKE OATMEAL, WHOLE-GRAIN BREADS & CEREALS

oh Boy.

Kate's Country Friends™ WORK-OUT*

Lay down flat on back. Try to squeeze lumpy thighs & fat rear-end into minute spandex tights... a work-out in itself.

☆

Reach! Stretch! Feel the burn as you try to get that box of cookies off the top shelf!

☆

Now rest... 1·2·3 ···· rest··· 1·2·3.

Now - don't you feel great?

* THIS WORK-OUT IS NOT SANCTIONED BY GOOSEBERRY PATCH

ACT Like A KID AGAIN

Ever notice how much energy kids have? Relive your childhood and revive your energy level!

Skip rope

play jacks

Swing on a tire

make mud pies

Jump in a puddle

DRAW with CHALK

YOUR MAJESTY'S S·C·H·E·D·U·L·E

1. Sleep in late.

2. Have your loyal subjects deliver brunch in bed. Read the paper.

3. Retire to the spa (the BATHROOM).

4. Indulge in Queenly pastimes including:

TREAT YOUR TOOTSIES TO A Pedicure.

THY ROYAL BUBBLE BATH BECKONS.

A FACIAL, OF COURSE.

TRY THE WHOLE ARRAY OF CONDITIONERS & LOTIONS.

A MANICURE, WHOLE BODY EXFOLIATING SCRUB, OR A WAXING IS A WELL-DESERVED TREAT.

5. Slip into your comfiest lounging clothes.

6. Treat yourself to something yummy.

7. Read, sleep, relax!

125

♥ other ♥ Royal treats

♥ send yourself flowers

♥ a cozy quilted bed jacket

♥ a satin eye mask

♥ silky satin sheets & a down-filled Comforter

♥ toasty lamb's wool throw

♥ china teapot & teacup

Yummy

♥ bon-bons

♥ a nice bedtray

"Rank does not confer privilege or give power. It imposes responsibility."
—Peter Drucker—

You may want to go out on your balcony and wave your royal sceptor at your neighbors.

Ring your little silver bell for

The Queen's Lunch

ALL-RIGHT!

♥ Minted Tea ♥ Sandwiches

1 c. mayonnaise
2 T. sour cream
1 T. lemon zest
2 t. coarse-grained mustard
2 t. fresh lemon juice
24 thin-sliced white bread
1 c. mint leaves
16 radishes, sliced very thin

♥

In a bowl, stir together mayonnaise, sour cream, zest, mustard, lemon juice, salt & pepper to taste. Spread on bread. Top 12 slices with layer of mint, then top mint with rows of radish slices. Top with remaining slices of bread. Cut sandwiches in half diagonally. (makes 24 sandwiches to share with kitchen staff.)

♥ Sliced Mango
♥ Rosemary Tea

Begin with a sprig of fresh rosemary. Put it in a teacup with a bag of your favorite tea. Pour in boiling water ~ allow to steep.

OFF WITH HER HEAD !!

SHE NEGLECTED TO TRIM THE CRUSTS OFF MY TEA SANDWICH!

127

♡ Indulge in ♡

Romance

Turn down the lights.

Send a love letter.

Draw a lipstick heart on the bathroom mirror.

Take a moonlight stroll hand-in-hand.

Have a winter picnic in front of the fireplace.

Go on a date.

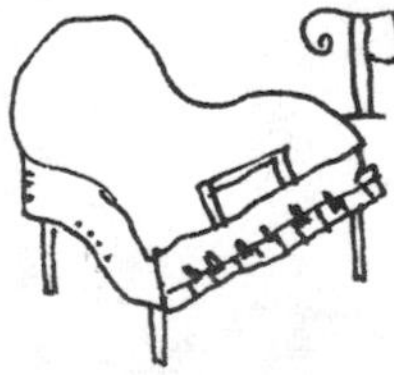

Play the piano together.

Sit on a big hill and gaze out.

At the touch of love, everyone becomes a poet.

~ PLATO ~

The best way to make your dreams come true is to wake up. ～J.M.POWER～

CHAPTER 7:

Wildest Dreams

The Country Friends™ dream on and on and on...

5 Sweet Country Friends™ you see, so quiet and so mild, but look a little DEEPER, friend, and you'll find something WILD.

I Would if I Could...

* DIVE

* FLY

* BE A COWGIRL IN THE WILD WILD WEST

Yes, I Would! if I could I sure would!

* BE AN OLYMPIC SNOWBOARDER

* DANCE SWAN LAKE

Yes! I Would...

131

* Hot Air Ballooning

* Hang Gliding

...Learn to soar and fly away!

* Sky Diving

* Bungee Jumping

133

...I'd swim with the dolphins in the sea...

*Scuba diving

...Climb way up high for a good look-see.

*mountain Climbing

I'd eat some squid, perhaps some snails...

*Gourmet Dining

...speed down a mountain (on my tail).

*Snow Skiing

135

I WOULD TRAVEL

I'd make my plans and pack my bag

jump on a train~ (avoid jet lag)

I'd see the sights from Sea to Bay as I'd swing across the *U·S·A*.

HELLO from the ATLANTIC

WISH YOU WERE HERE IN SAN FRANCISCO

things to See:

* YELLOWSTONE
* GRAND CANYON
* WASHINGTON D.C.
* EVERGLADES
* FALL LEAVES ON EAST COAST
* GRACELAND
* BIGGEST BALL OF ALUMINUM FOIL
* THE ROCKIES
* REDWOOD FOREST
* PAINTED DESERT
* APPALACHIANS
* BIG SKY MONTANA
* KANSAS PRAIRIES

OK, that's
done...
now where?

↓

I'd board a
plane,
fly through
the
air...

go 'round the
world &
see it all...
every single
port of
call.➥

Wanna know just where I'd go?
(here's my list, if you insist)

A cruise in the middle of winter

A visit to my ancestors' homeland

Tahiti, or some place equally exotic

PASS PORT

On a Safari in Kenya

To the bottom of the Grand Canyon on a mule train

Stay in a castle in Europe

On a walking tour in Ireland

OLD IRISH PROVERB:
MAY YOU LIVE ALL THE DAYS OF YOUR LIFE.

Well, upon having second thoughts...

I'll go back to school & teach some tots...

*Kindergarten teacher

...own a bed & breakfast place...

Holly's

...drive really fast, win every race!

*Demolition Derby driver

No, wait...I know just what I'll do...

Hold fast to dreams, for if dreams die,
life is a broken-winged bird
that cannot fly. ~Langston Hughes

143

Oh, how I wish...

I could sing & dance on the stage...

see JoAnn in "CATS"

★ Be in a Broadway musical

... be a go-go dancer in a cage!

★ Nightclub performer

I'd learn to tango in my loafers...

★ Ginger Rogers wanna-be

...play bass guitar for "The Gophers."

Rock & Roll Band member

145

Make a Crazy Wish!

I wish I had a million bucks.

I wish I had a trillion bucks.

I wish I had a dollar.

Money is a good servant but a bad master.

~ French proverb ~

Fondest Fantasies

I've always wanted to jump naked into a vat of chocolate pudding.

(do you find that odd?)

...RATED G!

I'm locked inside the dog treat plant overnight....

I'm a Beauty Contestant WINNER!

I Live on an island for a year — him Tarzan, me Jane!

OK, I'm walking into a garage sale, see, and I find a perfect set of 16 matched Windsor chairs, circa 1762, for $25 ··· on the way out, I happen to see an 1812 handmade red & white quilt for $3.··· and lo & behold if I don't uncover a beautiful blue saltglaze jug for 25¢! And when I get home, I find $80,000 stuffed inside the crock and a gold dubloon stitched inside··

What we need are more people who specialize in the impossible.
—THEODORE ROETHKE

147

And Let's Not Forget...

WINNING THE LOTTERY

BEING TRAPPED ON AN ELEVATOR WITH TOM CRUISE, TOM SELLECK & NO CHILDREN. (A VERY CROWDED ELEVATOR)

HAVING FUN WITH SOMEONE ELSE'S CREDIT CARDS.

COCOA WEAR

HOUSE OF ROCKS

HAVING HIGH TEA WITH THE QUEEN

BEING TALL & THIN!

HAVING CLEAVAGE!

If one is Lucky, a Solitary Fantasy can totaley transform one million Realities.
-MAYA ANGELOU

149

CHEAP THRILLS

WATCH THE SUNSET, AND THE MOONRISE.

GO FISHING~ CATCH A STORY ABOUT THE ONE THAT GOT AWAY!

FLY A KITE SO HIGH YOU CAN BARELY SEE IT.

SCREAM YOUR FOOL HEAD OFF ON A ROLLER COASTER!

HOLD HANDS UNDER THE TABLE AT A FRENCH CAFÉ. oui!

WATCH YOUR GARDEN GROW.

The moon belongs to ev'ryone,
the best things in life are free,
The stars belong to ev'ryone,
They gleam there for you & me.
-BUDDY DESYLVA-

The best
things
in life
are
not
free but
priceless.
~BENJAMIN LICHTENBERG~

RIDE THE
FERRIS
WHEEL
WITH
SOMEONE
YOU LOVE
AFTER DARK.

WATCH
YOUR KID
DO SOMETHING
GOOD!

Think big thoughts but relish SMALL pleasures. ~H. JACKSON BROWN

Every soul needs a D*R*E*A*M

Write Yours Here:

_____

_____

_____

_____

_____

_____

_____

_____

LATIN PROVERB:
Spoken words fly away; written words remain.

Live all you can; it's a mistake not to. It doesn't so much matter what you do in particular, so long as you have had your life. If you haven't had that, what have you had?

~ Henry James ~

One makes one's own happiness only by taking care of the happiness of others.
~ SAINT·PIERRE ~

LIFE-SIZE PLASTER ELVIS

HAPPY BiRTHDAY KATE!

CHAPTER 8:

Little Luxuries

Great Country Friends™ Gifts...

The hand that gives gathers.

-OLD ENGLISH PROVERB-

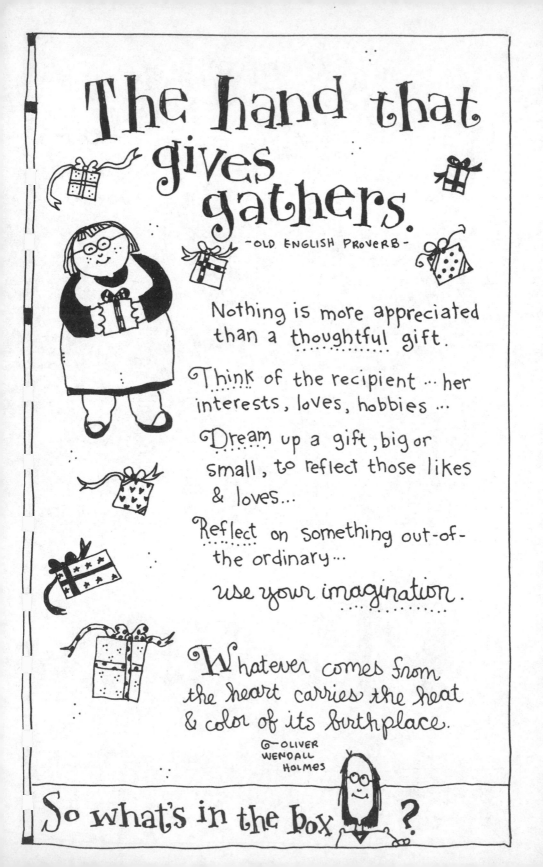

Nothing is more appreciated than a thoughtful gift.

Think of the recipient ... her interests, loves, hobbies ...

Dream up a gift, big or small, to reflect those likes & loves...

Reflect on something out-of-the ordinary...

use your imagination.

Whatever comes from the heart carries the heat & color of its birthplace.
— OLIVER WENDALL HOLMES

So what's in the box?

I JUST LOVE IT!

A BASKET GIFT IN A BASKET!

THAT'S RIGHT ∽ A GIFT BASKET FULL OF BASKET GIFTS... PERFECT FOR YOUR FAVORITE BASKET-LADY. (got it?)

FIND A WONDERFUL COLLECTABLE BASKET, OLD OR NEW. FILL 'ER UP WITH BASKET-THEMED GOODIES:

RECIPE CARDS DECORATED WITH BASKETS

TIN BASKET COOKIE CUTTER...

...REAL COOKIES MADE WITH A COOKIE CUTTER!

A BOX OF BASKET NOTE-CARDS

THE TINIEST BASKET YOU CAN FIND, STRUNG ON A SATIN RIBBON

"BASKETY" KITCHEN LINENS

A BASKET MAGNET

A SIGN

BASKET CASE

A PEWTER BASKET PIN

Just gimme 1 teensy hint.

157

Vickie's Tea·Lover's Basket

Line a basket with paper doilies ... add a tin of very special tea; homemade bread & preserves ... a lacy napkin & beautiful antique china teacup... and a pretty jar of Vickie's

Lemon Sugar

1 c. sugar   1 pkg. (.23 oz) unsweetened lemonade-flavored soft drink mix

Combine well & place in jar or cello bag tied tightly with ribbon.

∘₀∘∘₀∘

Gift Baskets don't have to begin with a basket! The Tea·Lover's Gift would also be wonderful all tucked in a pretty tin or a big old pitcher... just down-size the bread to tiny muffins.

C'mon... pleeeeze ?

THE
♥ Let·'em·eat·cake
Big BOWL o' GOODIES

···perfect for a shower gift!

Find a gigantic mixing bowl
& fill with everything a
cake·cook needs:

♥ CAKE MIX
♥ CANNED FROSTING
♥ KITCHEN TOWELS
♥ OVEN MITT
♥ MEASURING CUPS

♥ SPRINKLES
♥ SPATULA
♥ RECIPES HAND-
WRITTEN ON
CARDS

♥ CUPCAKE PAPER LINERS
♥ CAKE TESTER
♥ GIFT CERTIFICATE FOR
VANILLA ICE CREAM
♥ BIRTHDAY CANDLES

You tell how or
I'll throw A FIT.

159

A BLOOMIN' GOOD GARDEN GIFT

A thoughtful house-warmer, this collection of goodies might contain:

- seed packets
- gift certificate to a local nursery
- gardening magazines & subscriptions
- trowels
- garden gloves
- tulip bulbs
- garden shears
- plant markers
- watering can
- small potted herbs or flowers

Tuck everything in a huge clay pot — if the pot's big enough, add a rolled-up garden hose! You can rub paint on the pot for a worn look, or glue on old seed packets.

A big old plastic bucket also makes a handy holder.

DEAR TEACHER...

to Mr & Myers

A plain old brown-paper lunch bag will turn into a cherished gift bag with just a few easy tricks. Cut top of bag with big scallops. Add slits all around top of bag and thread a bright ribbon through holes. Before tying it shut, tuck an after-school treat inside for a favorite teacher... a shiny red apple & a jar of easy-to-make

APPLE DIP

I HELPED!

8-oz. pkg. cream cheese, softened
2 T. milk
1 t. vanilla
2 T. brown sugar
1 t. ground cinnamon
¼ t. ground nutmeg

Blend all ingredients together until smooth.

FOR PASTA LOVERS

...how about a colander complete with a jar of marinara sauce, pasta, olive oil, garlic bulbs & wine glasses? Add a C.D. of romantic violin music!

I'm assuming that gift's for me... RIGHT?

PIZZA BASKET

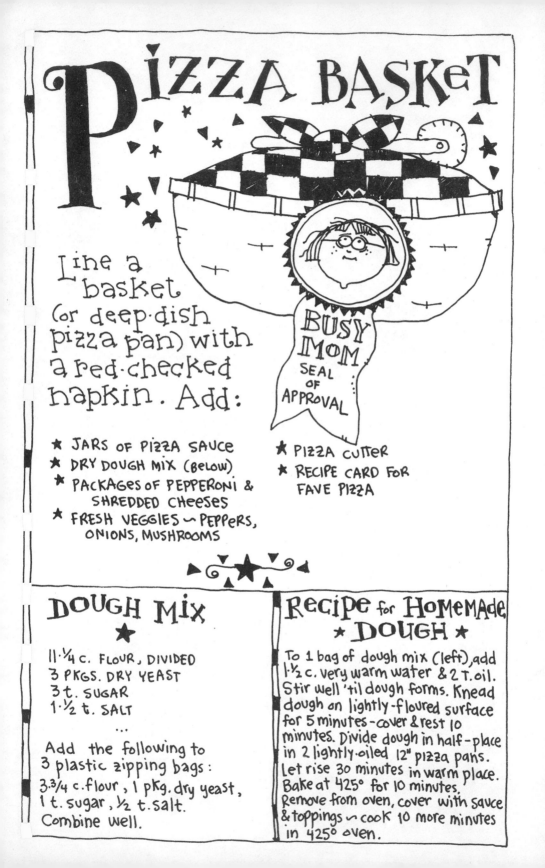

Line a basket (or deep-dish pizza pan) with a red-checked napkin. Add:

BUSY MOM SEAL OF APPROVAL

★ JARS OF PIZZA SAUCE
★ DRY DOUGH MIX (BELOW)
★ PACKAGES OF PEPPERONI & SHREDDED CHEESES
★ FRESH VEGGIES ~ PEPPERS, ONIONS, MUSHROOMS

★ PIZZA CUTTER
★ RECIPE CARD FOR FAVE PIZZA

DOUGH MIX
★

11·¼ c. FLOUR, DIVIDED
3 PKGS. DRY YEAST
3 t. SUGAR
1·½ t. SALT
...

Add the following to 3 plastic zipping bags:
3·¾ c. flour, 1 pkg. dry yeast, 1 t. sugar, ½ t. salt.
Combine well.

Recipe for Homemade ★ DOUGH ★

To 1 bag of dough mix (left), add 1·½ c. very warm water & 2 T. oil. Stir well 'til dough forms. Knead dough on lightly-floured surface for 5 minutes - cover & rest 10 minutes. Divide dough in half - place in 2 lightly-oiled 12" pizza pans. Let rise 30 minutes in warm place. Bake at 425° for 10 minutes. Remove from oven, cover with sauce & toppings ~ cook 10 more minutes in 425° oven.

OTHER GIFT BASKET ideas

FOR A BOOK LOVER:

A STACK OF NEWLY-RELEASED PAPERBACKS... A BOOKMARK... BOOKPLATES & A BOOKLIGHT

...in a neat BOOK BAG!

(Literally - a wonderful gift!)

FOR A GOLF ADDICT:

BEGIN WITH A GOLF HAT, TURNED UPSIDE DOWN...

... FILL IT UP WITH SHREDDED GRASS. PLANT A LAYER OF COLORFUL TEES, THEN A LAYER OF GOLF BALLS.

HOT GLUE A LITTLE CANARY ON THE BRIM OF THE HAT.

(A BIRDIE - GET IT?)

FOR THE FISHING Fanatic ON YOUR LIST:

FIND A SMALL TREE BRANCH. MOUNT IT ON A BLOCK OF PINE SO IT LOOKS LIKE A MINIATURE DEAD TREE. TANGLE SNARLS OF FISHING LINE, NEW FISHING LURES & BOBBERS IN THE TREE FOR A FISHERMAN'S DELIGHT.

"You may give gifts without CARING ~ but you can't care without giving."

-Frank A. Clark-

163

Charming Baby gifts

...nothing essential, just essentially *wonderful*.

♥ Baby's cup, made of the finest china

The softest blankie imaginable

♥ Personalized Thank You notes, printed with baby's name

A very good collectable stuffed toy ...perhaps a Steiff?

A wonderful frame

♥ A keepsake sterling locket engraved with baby's name & birthdate

♥ A beautiful lullaby CD

A hand-painted toybox for baby's room

You are the trip I did not take;
You are the pearls
        I cannot buy;
You are my blue Italian lake;
You are my piece of foreign sky.

—"To my child" Anne Campbell, 1888

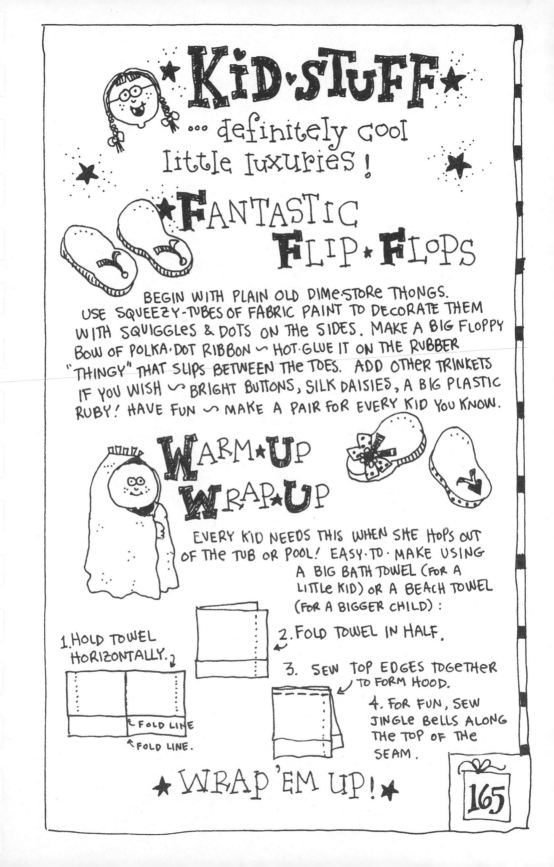

★ KID ★ STUFF ★

... definitely cool little luxuries!

★ FANTASTIC FLIP ★ FLOPS

BEGIN WITH PLAIN OLD DIME·STORE THONGS. USE SQUEEZY·TUBES OF FABRIC PAINT TO DECORATE THEM WITH SQUIGGLES & DOTS ON THE SIDES. MAKE A BIG FLOPPY BOW OF POLKA·DOT RIBBON ∿ HOT·GLUE IT ON THE RUBBER "THINGY" THAT SLIPS BETWEEN THE TOES. ADD OTHER TRINKETS IF YOU WISH ∿ BRIGHT BUTTONS, SILK DAISIES, A BIG PLASTIC RUBY! HAVE FUN ∿ MAKE A PAIR FOR EVERY KID YOU KNOW.

WARM ★ UP WRAP ★ UP

EVERY KID NEEDS THIS WHEN SHE HOPS OUT OF THE TUB OR POOL! EASY·TO·MAKE USING A BIG BATH TOWEL (FOR A LITTLE KID) OR A BEACH TOWEL (FOR A BIGGER CHILD):

1. HOLD TOWEL HORIZONTALLY.

← FOLD LINE
← FOLD LINE.

2. FOLD TOWEL IN HALF.

3. SEW TOP EDGES TOGETHER TO FORM HOOD.

4. FOR FUN, SEW JINGLE BELLS ALONG THE TOP OF THE SEAM.

★ WRAP 'EM UP! ★

make a BABY QUILT
for a new mommy

Have friends gather & do it the old-fashioned way ... by hand! Get together, gossip, laugh ... and sew. Each friend can cross-stitch a square, or non-sewers can stencil or hand-paint their panel.

Gear your design to a nursery theme (Mary Elizabeth's baby room had a farm animal border), or have each friend put a special thought, prayer or message on her square.

Whatever design you choose, mother & child will cherish such a lovely & personal keepsake.

A baby is such a nice way to start a person.

go for a group Make ✫ over

~ definitely a luxury! ~

Can you even imagine the possibilities? ➤

BEFORE

OPTION #1. Put together a home spa and invite the girls over for a relaxing afternoon of manicures, facials & pampering.

OPTION #2. Make an appointment with your hometown salon for the works... and take everybody with you! Mudpacks, massages & manicures all around...not to mention new 'dos!

OPTION #3. Save your mad money and check en mass into a luxury spa. Three days of gourmet food and seaweed scrubs never killed anyone.

167

Hmmm... Grandma's Birthday...

WHAT TO GET FOR SOMEONE WHO DOESN'T NEED ANYTHING?

I love it!

♥ Put together an entire outfit ~ layer each article between pretty tissue in a decorated box! A sweater... blouse... skirt... scarf... stockings... necklace... earrings... perfume... *what fun!*

♥ Fill a brand-new purse with all kinds of treasures: a keyring... sunglasses... wallet... mirror... hand lotion... hankie... *everything she needs!*

WHAT on EartH can I get him?

I need socks.

★ Men can be so hard to buy for! Give the gift of your time: do his least favorite chores~ mowing, washing the car, shining his shoes.

★ Buy him a hammock to nap in, or an extra-comfy lawn chair for the back yard.

★ Dad & Grandpa will love a photo frame with your favorite picture of the 2 of you together in it.

★ You can't go wrong with something home-baked!

---

a wonderful gift for someone who TRAVELS *a lot...*

Make an extravagant velvet shoe bag for her. It's a treat she wouldn't buy herself. Make it roomy, and close it with a zipper or drawstring.

Cool. I wear a 9½. JUST IN CASE YOU WANT TO BUY ME SHOES, TOO.

Little Luxuries
for
♥ Kids, ♥
Both Big & Little!

Keep a good stack of sketchpads, paints & pencils on hand for your kids... encourage creativity & imagination!

Art supplies make a great gift, too, for little kids... and adults, too. Everyone has a creative urge ∽ pack a toolbox or craft carrier with a good selection of art supplies, and give it to your favorite aspiring Rembrandt:

★ SKETCHPADS   ★ BRUSHES   ★ CANVASSES
★ WATERCOLORS   ★ COLORED   ★ OIL PAINTS
★ CRAYONS   PENCILS   ★ RULER
★ MARKERS   ★ PASTELS   ★ SCISSORS
★ GUM ERASER   ★ PALETTES   ★ NEAT PAPERS   ★ GLUE

PLAY IT AGAIN!

Listen to the music... take music lessons! You're never too old. Learn piano, harmonica or banjo ∽

music is a life-long pleasure.

171

How we Love The Little Luxuries from Old Mother Nature

♥ Someone who lives in a house with no gardening space would surely love a **Portable Herb garden!** Fill a small red wagon with pots of rosemary, basil & peppermint, and roll it right onto the patio.

Dried Oranges

♥ oh, what a fragrant gift! Cut 8 thin wedge-shaped pieces from the peel of an orange. Let the orange stay in a warm, dry spot for several weeks — as it dries, the cuts will widen. Pretty, fragrant, & easier to make than a pomander!

♥ Fold down the sides of a pretty lunch-size gift bag & drop in a bright pot of geraniums for an easy-to-deliver **Spirit Lifter.** (Slit the corners of the bag about 3" down from the top to make the fold).

♥ A small **Tree** makes a thoughtful gift to commemorate a marriage, new baby or housewarming. Choose one at your local nursery or give a gift certificate.

A marvelous way to share memories...

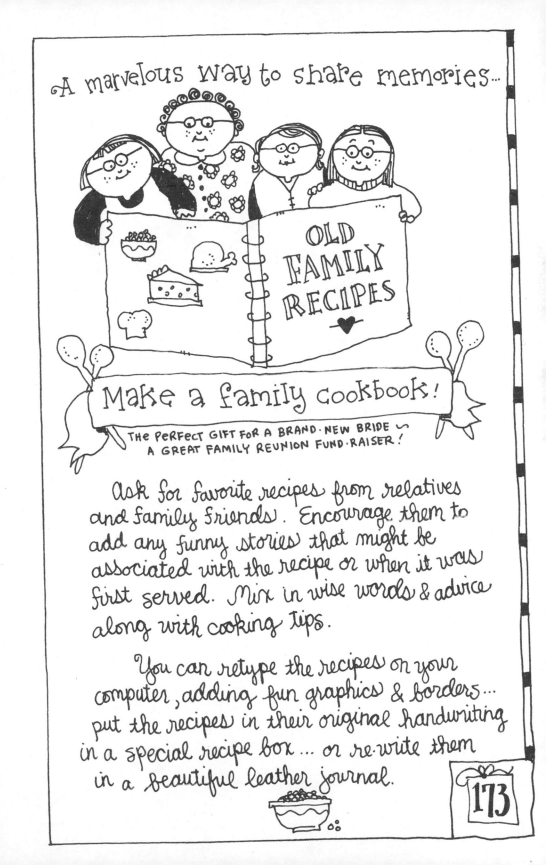

OLD FAMILY RECIPES ♥

Make a family cookbook!

THE PERFECT GIFT FOR A BRAND·NEW BRIDE ~
A GREAT FAMILY REUNION FUND·RAISER!

Ask for favorite recipes from relatives and family friends. Encourage them to add any funny stories that might be associated with the recipe or when it was first served. Mix in wise words & advice along with cooking tips.

You can retype the recipes on your computer, adding fun graphics & borders... put the recipes in their original handwriting in a special recipe box... or re-write them in a beautiful leather journal.

Creature Comforts

Doesn't __everyone__ have 7 dogs & 3 cats? You say you don't? Then it's time to invite at least one four-legged friend to share your life. Animals bring unconditional love and companionship to a relationship ⌣ find out for yourself (or just ask Spotty!).

If you can't have an animal companion, offer to volunteer at a shelter. Your local humane society not only needs homes for cats and dogs, but volunteers too!

Country Friends™ Special Friends Treats

2·½ c. whole wheat flour
½ c. non-fat dry milk
1 t. sugar
1 t. salt
6 T. butter
1 egg

Mix all ingredients together with ½ c. cold water. Knead for 3 minutes, then roll out to ½" thickness. Cut with bone-shaped cutter for dogs & fish-shaped cutter for cats. Bake on lightly-oiled cookie sheet for 30 minutes at 350°.

Use the same cutters to make black construction paper shapes ∽ glue paper bones & fish on a brown paper lunch bag. Tuck the treats inside & glue bag shut. Punch hole in center of bag top ∽ use raffia to thread through hole & tie the cookie cutters to the bag...

a special treat for your favorite animal lover!

175

CHAPTER 9:

Free Time

Time & tide wait for no man.
— CHAUCER —

Free Time: Getting it and Spending It...

Each day is a little life;
    every waking & rising a little birth;
every fresh morning a little youth.....
                            – Arthur Schopenhauer

MAKE IT A

Good Morning

Focus on beginning your day off SLOW...
instead of running around, slamming doors & looking
for lost shoes, start off in a *peaceful* way.
Gently wake everyone with a tender back rub or
in a playful way with the family pet.

Gather books,
clothes & important
stuff before you go
to bed so the
morning routine doesn't
turn into a mad rush.

6 Morning Madness Sanity Savers

HoHUM!

Make a list & consult it!

Wake up 1 hour earlier every other day.

Take a minute to stretch... first thing!

Fix lunchboxes & lunchbags the night before.

Delegate a morning rush chore to each child — fill juice glasses, let Spotty out, pick up the newspaper.

Buy a keyrack... and use it!

good morning RITUALS

Make time for an everyday ritual ~ it's a pleasant pause between waking up & venturing out into the world for your children, and a small pleasure for parents:

♥ read the morning funny papers together

♥ make a wish or say a short prayer for a good day at school and work

♥ Rub noses; an "eskimo kiss" is a nice send-off to the school bus!

♥ Ask the kids what they dreamed of last night... an interesting way to start the day!

♥ TAKE THE TIME ♥

ON GETTING ORGANIZED:
☆
create a
☆ KIDS' ☆
CABINET

Designate a cabinet or cupboard or closet by the door just for the kids' junk: book bags, homework, mittens, lunchboxes... all the stuff you can never find as the schoolbus pulls up in the driveway.

In a perfect world, this might work.

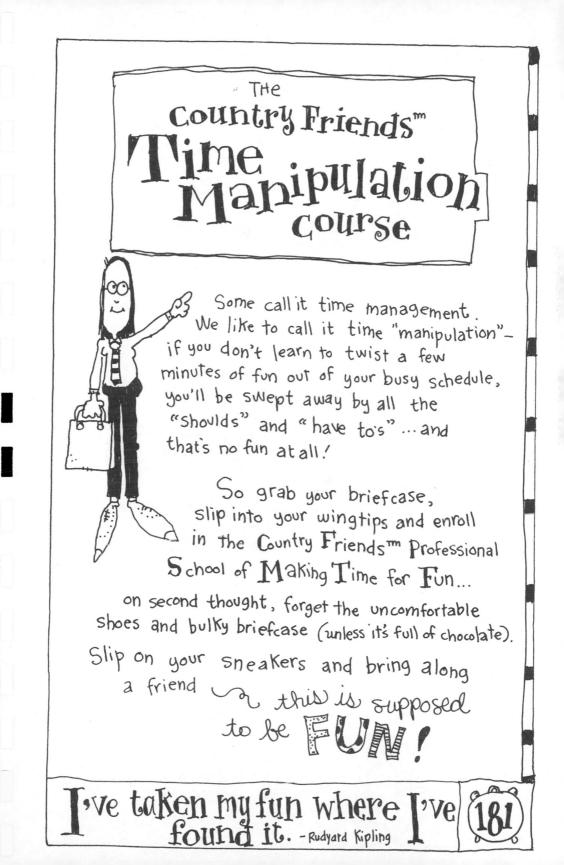

"The
Country Friends™
Time
Manipulation
course

Some call it time management.
We like to call it time "manipulation"—
if you don't learn to twist a few
minutes of fun out of your busy schedule,
you'll be swept away by all the
"shoulds" and "have to's" ...and
that's no fun at all!

So grab your briefcase,
slip into your wingtips and enroll
in the Country Friends™ Professional
School of Making Time for Fun...

on second thought, forget the uncomfortable
shoes and bulky briefcase (unless it's full of chocolate).

Slip on your sneakers and bring along
a friend ～ *this is supposed*
to be **FUN!**

I've taken my fun where I've
found it. – Rudyard Kipling

181

Learn to say NO.

"certainly! I'd love to chair the Committee for Making More Rules."

You'll reap big time rewards right away if you can say "no" gracefully. No need to make excuses; just tell the truth — you're already over-committed and one more job means less time for your family.

A CANCELLED DENTIST APPOINTMENT

KID WITH TONSILLITUS

DOG POOPED ON RUG

I FORGOT TO BUY MILK

NEW DEAD-LINE: TODAY

Be Flexible.

Keep yourself centered. If something unexpected throws you off schedule, don't go to pieces. Use the time to your advantage, or go with the flow... don't panic.

Focus.

Do just one thing at a time and give it all your attention. You'll finish faster with a better end-result.

Delegate.

Nobody can do it all by herself.

Enjoy the un-enjoyable.

You know that old saying, "Time flies when you're having fun"... it's true! Every day brings some task you don't look forward to; make the most of it. Sing while you do the dishes. Dance as you vacuum. Whistle as you scrub the tub.

You'll look like you're having so much fun maybe the kids will join in. (but don't count on it)

Time flies whether you're having fun or not.

Don'T worry.

It's a colossal waste of time. It causes wrinkles. Just don't do it.

Let's see, I know there's a spoon in here somewhere....

A few dirty dishes in the sink won't kill you.

So let 'em sit tonight and play with your kids instead. (*Exceptions to this rule:

1. Can you say "SALMONELLA"? When dishes in sink start to resemble a biology experiment, it's time to load the dishwasher.

2. When the E.P.A. or local health department official comes to your kitchen door, it's time to wash the dishes.

3. When you run out of plates, forks & glasses, it's time to run some hot water in the sink.)

Child Welfare won't take your kids away if they don't have a green veggie at EVERY MEAL.

MY BABIES!

Eat fast food every once in a while.
You'll get a break and your kids will love it.

I CAN'T LOOK.

So WHAT if you don't make the bed every morning?

Loosen Up!

185

Cleanliness is next to impossible.
-PHYLLIS DILLER

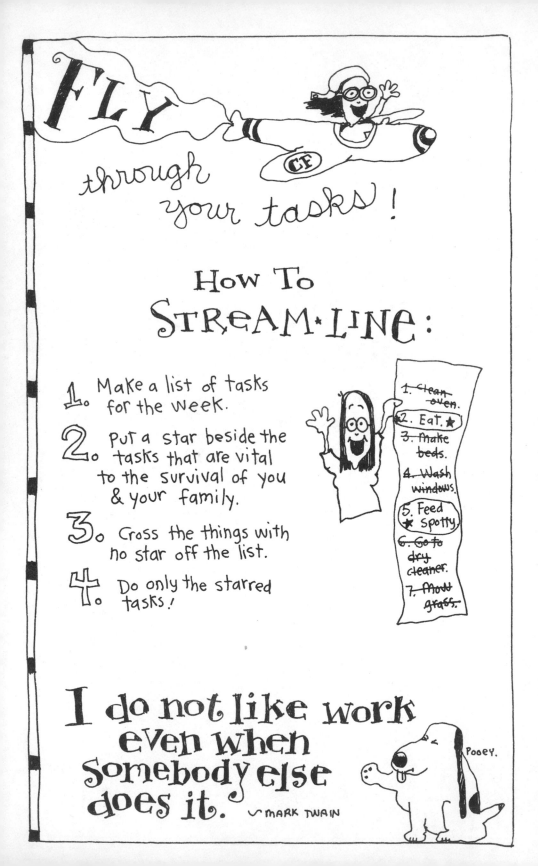

FLY

through your tasks!

How To STREAM·LINE:

1. Make a list of tasks for the week.

2. Put a star beside the tasks that are vital to the survival of you & your family.

3. Cross the things with no star off the list.

4. Do only the starred tasks!

1. Clean oven.
2. Eat. ★
3. make beds.
4. Wash windows.
5. Feed ★ Spotty
6. Go to dry cleaner.
7. mow grass.

"I do not like work even when somebody else does it." ~MARK TWAIN

Pooey.

TIME is SLIPPERY.
— KIM LINDER —

TIME WASTERS vs. **TIME SAVERS**

TV REMOTES …you'll watch TV longer than you should.

VIDEOTAPES …tape 'em, cut out the commercials, watch 'em when you _do_ have time.

NEW & UNUSUAL DISHES… Kids won't eat Gourmet Eggplant & Sauerkraut Quiche & you'll waste time fixing it.

FAVORITE RECIPES… ensure kids will eat. Just sneak a new ingredient on their pizza once in a while to introduce new foods.

POOR PHONE HABITS… You'll be a slave to every phone sales person who calls while supper burns if you answer every call & "call waiting."

THE ANSWERING MACHINE… can be a real blessing when you are busy. Screen your calls!

OVERSCHEDULED KIDS… too many lessons & activities will burn everyone out.

PRIORITIES…cut back to activities your child _really_ enjoys.

187

LET'S GO SHOPPING

(BUT LET'S MAKE IT QUICK)

Make a shopping list before you go. Plan your meals.

Arrange coupons in a file or envelope so you can find the right one in a flash. (Nothing's worse than being in line behind someone sorting through 2017 coupons for that one 35¢ off Puffy-Soft Toilet Tissue offer).

Skip the superstores when time is short. Smaller stores aren't usually as busy ~ you'll get in & out faster.

Shop for groceries early in the morning or late at night to miss the crowds.

WHATEVER WILL SATISFY HUNGER IS GOOD FOOD.
—CHINESE PROVERB—

Kate's Shopping Hints

... GUARANTEED TO SAVE YOU TIME!

For more tips, just send 19.99 plus shipping & handling to me and I'll come do your shopping for you.

1. BUY THINGS YOU USE A LOT IN BULK... for instance, chocolate almond fudge ice cream, chocolate pudding & chocolate fudgesicles.

2. DON'T GO TO THE STORE UNTIL YOU DON'T HAVE ANYTHING IN THE FRIDGE BUT MUSTARD.

3. AVOID THE AISLES WHERE YOU'RE TEMPTED TO DALLY... the magazine racks are deadly; The candy display can delay me for weeks.

CHOCO BAR

CANDY Ps & Qs

GUM

Vickie & JoAnn's Very Favorite Time-Saving Tip:

Purchase gifts through mail-order catalogs rather than taking time to go to a mall!

I believe the art of living consists not so much in complicating simple things as in simplifying things that are not. — François Hertel

a minute full o' fun

SQUEEZE IN 60 SECONDS OF RELAXATION OR FUN WHERE YOU CAN... SEIZE THE MOMENT!

★

GRAB A TABLOID at the MARKET WHILE YOU'RE WAITING IN LINE TO CHECK OUT.

ELVIS SPOTTING — ALIENS LOVE

★

GIVE YOURSELF A MINUTE MASSAGE at the STOP. LIGHT : PUT YOUR HEAD ON THE STEERING WHEEL. USING BOTH HANDS, GENTLY RUB THE BASE OF YOUR NECK WHERE IT MEETS YOUR SPINE.

★

CALL A FRIEND ON YOUR CAR PHONE WHILE YOU'RE 23RD IN LINE AT THE BURGER WORLD DRIVE-THRU.

DAYDREAM WHILE YOU'RE ON HOLD.

Glorious ways to spend your coins of Time

Time is the coin of your life.

It is the only coin you have, and only you can determine how it will be spent. Be careful lest you let other people spend it for you.

— CARL SANDBURG

Small Change

Hit a Tennis Ball against the garage door.

Watch the clouds or look at the stars.

Enjoy the quiet during those few minutes before everyone else gets up in the morning.

Enjoy a savory dessert— eat a piece of chocolate cream pie or chomp cookies in milk.

ALBUM

Look through family photos.

1 MILLION SMACKERS

Test drive a car completely out of your price range.

Go to bed early!

Take a walk with the dog.

Re·pot something green.

Re·arrange the furniture.

hi.

Play on the Internet.

hello old pal

Write a letter to a far-away friend.

Meditate or pray.

Go window-shopping.

The little things of life are as interesting as the big ones. ~THOREAU

191

COUNTRY FRIENDS™ other ideas:

I'D PAINT A MURAL ON THE KIDS' BEDROOM WALL.

We the people.

CROSS·STITCH THE CONSTITUTION INTO A 12·FOOT· SQUARE WALL HANGING.

COOK OR BAKE: IT'S FUN WHEN WE DON'T HAVE TO DO IT!

VOLUNTEER AT A NURSING HOME.

Hello Dear.

CHECK INTO A BED & BREAKFAST FOR SOME REAL RELAXATION.

Have Fun.

WE'D PLAN A BIG OLD PARTY!

I'D CUT 214 STROKES OFF MY GAME.

STENCIL THE PORCH FLOOR.

CATCH UP ON SOME GOOD FICTION.

Serve Others.

BUILD A STONE WALL.

VISIT MY FRIEND CAROL MORE REGULARLY.

LEARN CALLIGRAPHY.

Learn something new.

I'D PLANT AN HERB GARDEN BY MY BACK DOOR.

193

Free Time: A breath of fresh air!

Spend an hour or so out-side...

Take a walk on the wild side with a child—you'll see things you haven't noticed for years. Spiderwebs, birdnests, anthills... Mother Nature's miracles!

Just look at all the different animals you can see on your walk... isn't it amazing? Kids can spin a mighty yarn about all these creatures that share your neighborhood. Encourage the tale-telling as you walk!

Look for Big Foot!

"...though we should be grateful for good houses, there is, after all, no house like God's out-of-doors."

~Robert Louis Stevenson~

Make a home-made WATER SCOPE: Cut off the bottom of a plastic milk jug. Cover it tightly with clear plastic kitchen wrap, using rubber bands to secure it. Hold your water scope a few inches under water & look through the top hole at all the life under the water at your local pond!

Sit by pond's edge at sundown and just listen to all the nature sounds.

Lay down in the grass and look closely at the flowers.

...doing nothing in particular. It's the best kind of free time.

Black earth turned into yellow crocus is undiluted hocus-pocus.
~Piet Hein

195

Free timE:
Reading

once upon a time,

OH, THE PURE LUXURY OF A QUIET AFTERNOON WITH A REALLY GOOD BOOK!

I love to wander through a bookstore, thumbing through cookbooks.
~ Holly

Big, beautiful photo books with pictures of the sea, lighthouses, sailboats... aaah!
- JoAnn

I'd love to have time to read the classics... Treasure Island, Tom Sawyer, For whom the Bell Tolls....
~ Mary Elizabeth

Give me a big stack of magazines and I'm happy. (I read 'em back to front, you know — is that weird?)
— Vickie

I like to sit in the children's section of the library & look at the fairy tale books.
- Kate

BOOKS MAY BE THE ONLY TRUE MAGIC.
- ALICE HOFFMAN -

CHAPTER 10

E ast, west, home is best.
—H.A. BOHN—

Nesting

The
Country Friends™
show how
to make your home
as comfy as an old
easy chair...

Warm and Welcome Touches

to make a house a home

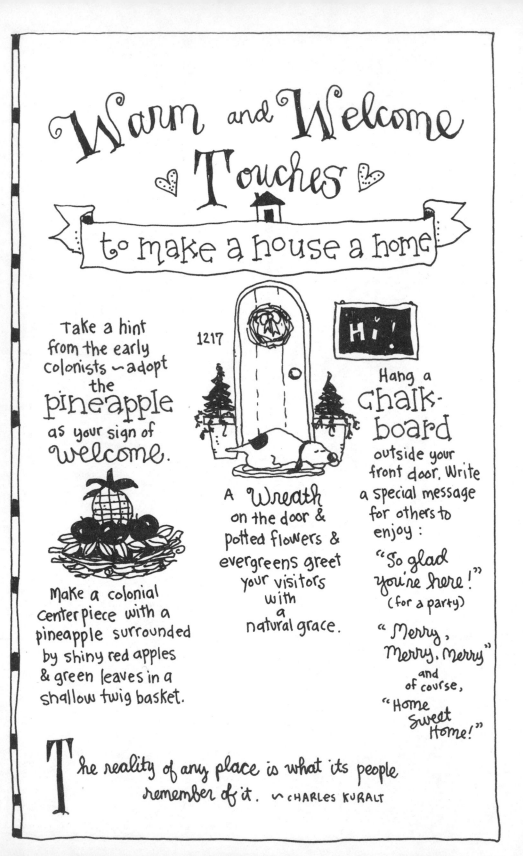

Take a hint from the early colonists ~ adopt the **pineapple** as your sign of **welcome.**

Make a colonial centerpiece with a pineapple surrounded by shiny red apples & green leaves in a shallow twig basket.

1217

Hi!

A **Wreath** on the door & potted flowers & evergreens greet your visitors with a natural grace.

Hang a **chalk-board** outside your front door. Write a special message for others to enjoy:

"So glad you're here!" (for a party)

"Merry, Merry, Merry" and of course, "Home Sweet Home!"

The reality of any place is what its people remember of it. ~ CHARLES KURALT

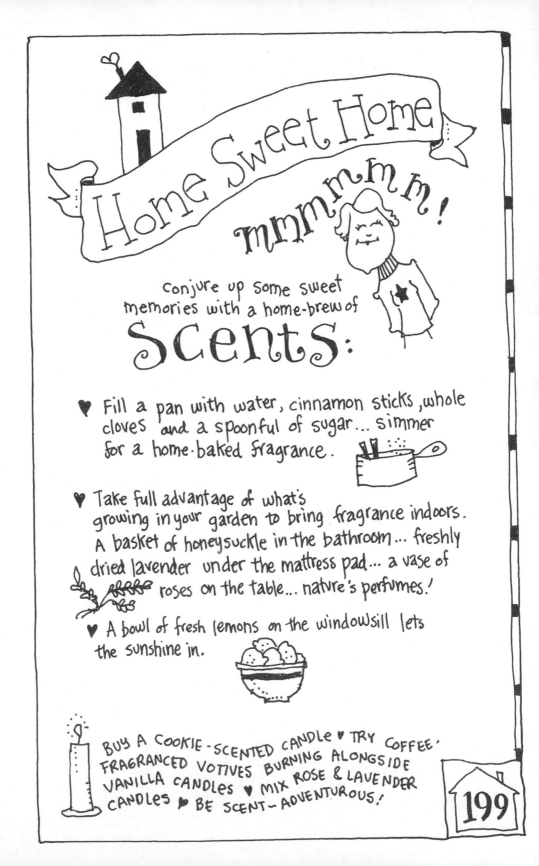

Home Sweet Home

mmmmmm!

conjure up some sweet memories with a home-brew of

SCENTS:

♥ Fill a pan with water, cinnamon sticks, whole cloves and a spoonful of sugar... simmer for a home-baked fragrance.

♥ Take full advantage of what's growing in your garden to bring fragrance indoors. A basket of honeysuckle in the bathroom... freshly dried lavender under the mattress pad... a vase of roses on the table... nature's perfumes!

♥ A bowl of fresh lemons on the windowsill lets the sunshine in.

BUY A COOKIE-SCENTED CANDLE ♥ TRY COFFEE-FRAGRANCED VOTIVES BURNING ALONGSIDE VANILLA CANDLES ♥ MIX ROSE & LAVENDER CANDLES ♥ BE SCENT-ADVENTUROUS!

199

What smells so WONDERFUL?

♥ Run out of votives? No more potpourri? When all else fails...

Bake Somethin'!

our favorite home-baked scents:

Cinnamon Rolls!

Nothin' beats sugar cookies right outta the oven.

Chocolate cake rules.

Baked apples win, hands-down!

Bread smells so ... comforting.

PIZZA!

Open the WINDOWS!

WINTER MORNINGS & SUMMER EVENINGS ~ THROW UP THE SASH AND TAKE A DEEP BREATH OF

FRESH AIR.

Put empty perfume bottles in your sock drawers. ♥ Tuck a sachet in between the towels in your linen closet. ♥ Light bulb rings filled with fragrance oil really work.

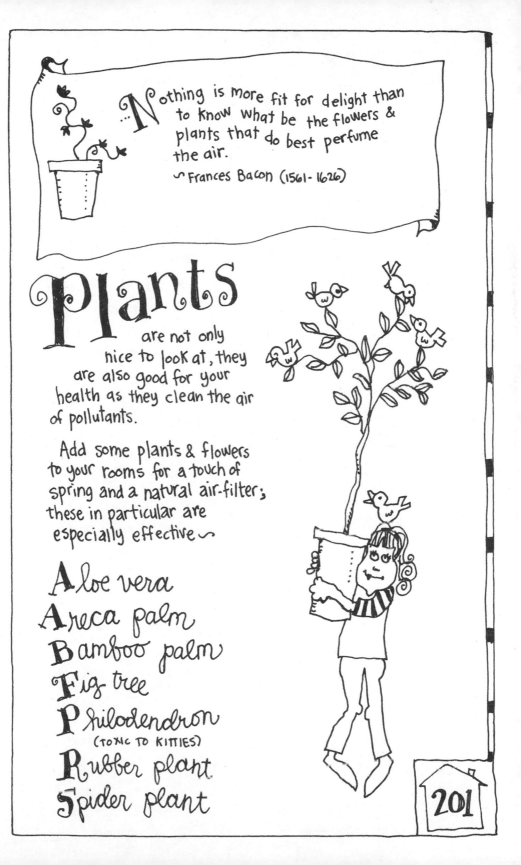

"...Nothing is more fit for delight than to know what be the flowers & plants that do best perfume the air.
～Frances Bacon (1561-1626)

Plants

are not only nice to look at, they are also good for your health as they clean the air of pollutants.

Add some plants & flowers to your rooms for a touch of spring and a natural air-filter; these in particular are especially effective～

Aloe vera
Areca palm
Bamboo palm
Fig tree
Philodendron
(TOXIC TO KITTIES)
Rubber plant
Spider plant

Spotty Speaks
on making a house a HomE

1. Sniff around.

2. Climb on the furniture if they'll let you. If not...

3. Find a warm spot – the floor by the window is nice.

4. Walk around the spot several times, round & round.

5. Now change directions; chase your tail in a tight circle in that one spot... slowly.

6. Collapse in a heap.

7. Smack your lips. Heave a happy sigh. This is home.

Find your own warm SPoT

Make your own favorite place at home with just a few simple ingredients:

♥ over-stuffed chair with ottoman
♥ snugly throw & cushy pillow
♥ reading lamp
♥ stack of good books
♥ small table to hold a cup o' tea
♥ doggy to lay at your feet

Aaaahh

Your home is an
extension of

YOU.

Decorate
it with
the
things

YOU
LOVE.

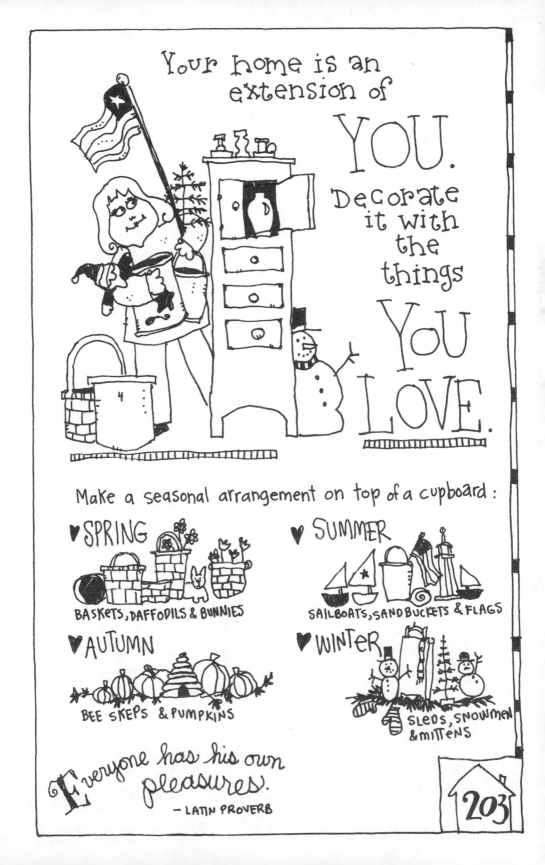

Make a seasonal arrangement on top of a cupboard:

♥ SPRING

BASKETS, DAFFODILS & BUNNIES

♥ SUMMER

SAILBOATS, SANDBUCKETS & FLAGS

♥ AUTUMN

BEE SKEPS & PUMPKINS

♥ WINTER

SLEDS, SNOWMEN & MITTENS

Everyone has his own pleasures.

— LATIN PROVERB

203

Use the things you Love...

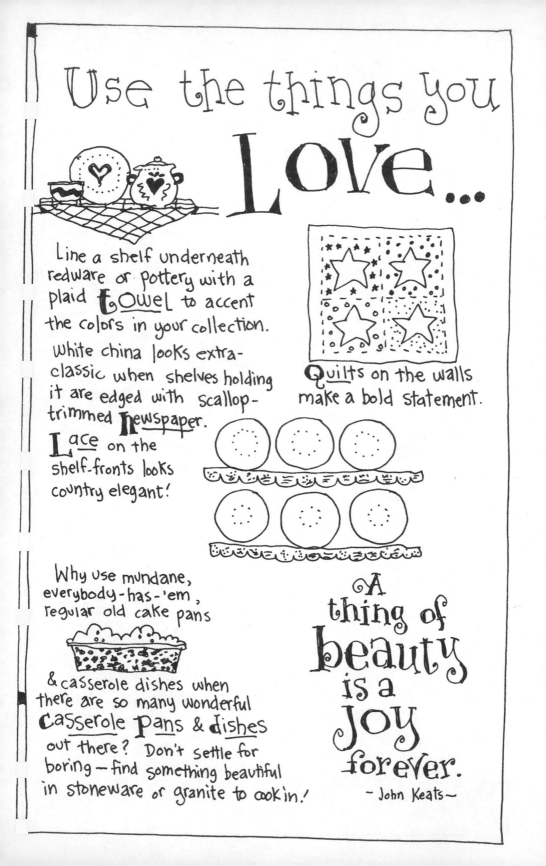

Line a shelf underneath redware or pottery with a plaid towel to accent the colors in your collection.

White china looks extra-classic when shelves holding it are edged with scallop-trimmed newspaper.

Lace on the shelf-fronts looks country elegant!

Quilts on the walls make a bold statement.

Why use mundane, everybody-has-'em, regular old cake pans & casserole dishes when there are so many wonderful casserole pans & dishes out there? Don't settle for boring — find something beautiful in stoneware or granite to cook in!

A thing of beauty is a joy forever.
~ John Keats ~

...Just use them differently!

★ Mary Elizabeth collects yellow ware bowls, and uses them on a shelf in the bathroom to store white & yellow washcloths, soaps & lotions.

★ Holly has a wonderful big old basket that is ALWAYS on her entryway table, summer or winter. It always looks different from season to season, though, as she fills it with something interesting and unique:

▲ SPRING: COLORFUL POOL BALLS & CROQUET BALLS

▲ SUMMER: HEDGEBALLS, GREEN & WONDERFULLY BUMPY!

▲ WINTER: DOZENS OF SINGLE MITTENS COLLECTED FROM FRIENDS

▲ AUTUMN: HUNDREDS OF ACORNS, WALNUTS & PECANS IN THEIR BEAUTIFUL SHELLS

★ Kate can't resist benches, but has a good use for them: She stacks them on top of each other and stores books on each other "shelf".

When you've got it... flaunt it!
~ George Lois

205

Picture This!

■ create a fresh new look by changing pictures around on the wall ... or even from room to room.

■ Collect old frames at garage sales & antique shows. Find similar ones or very different styles ... use them in their original finish or paint them all the same color to tie them together visually.

■ Frame lace, quilt blocks or antique clothing for something unique.

■ Make a picture rail by mounting 2"x2" strips of wood to the wall with screws. Lean frames along the shelf.

Life is a great big canvas, and you should throw all the paint on it you can. ~DANNY KAYE

New Life for an Old Lamp

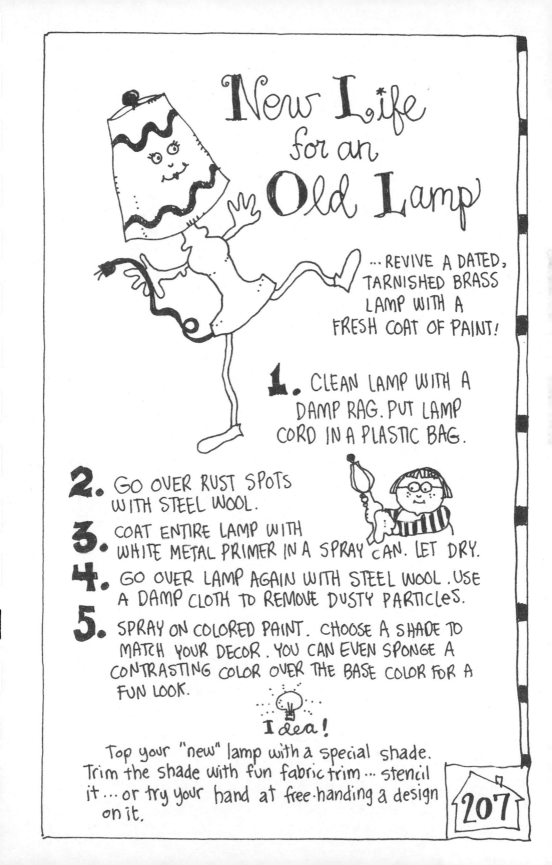

... REVIVE A DATED, TARNISHED BRASS LAMP WITH A FRESH COAT OF PAINT!

1. CLEAN LAMP WITH A DAMP RAG. PUT LAMP CORD IN A PLASTIC BAG.

2. GO OVER RUST SPOTS WITH STEEL WOOL.

3. COAT ENTIRE LAMP WITH WHITE METAL PRIMER IN A SPRAY CAN. LET DRY.

4. GO OVER LAMP AGAIN WITH STEEL WOOL. USE A DAMP CLOTH TO REMOVE DUSTY PARTICLES.

5. SPRAY ON COLORED PAINT. CHOOSE A SHADE TO MATCH YOUR DECOR. YOU CAN EVEN SPONGE A CONTRASTING COLOR OVER THE BASE COLOR FOR A FUN LOOK.

Idea!

Top your "new" lamp with a special shade. Trim the shade with fun fabric trim... stencil it... or try your hand at free-handing a design on it.

207

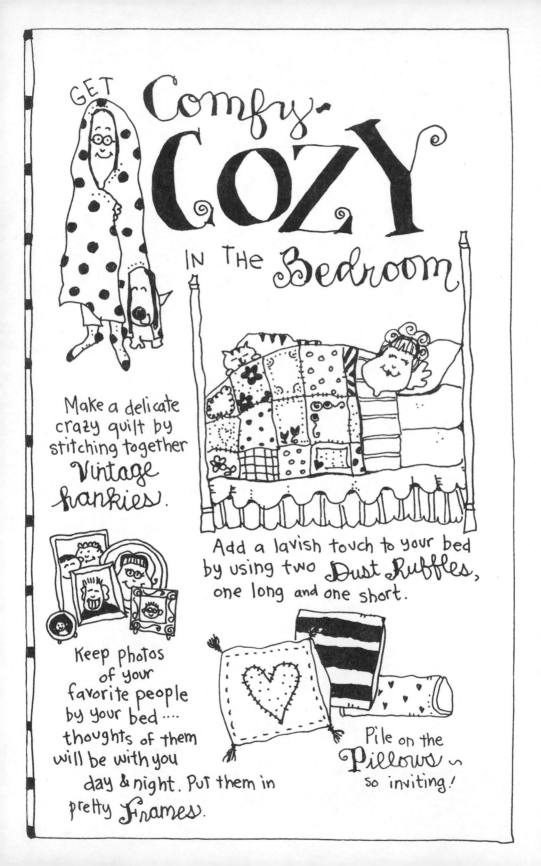

GET Comfy-
COZY
IN THE Bedroom

Make a delicate crazy quilt by stitching together Vintage hankies.

Add a lavish touch to your bed by using two Dust Ruffles, one long and one short.

Keep photos of your favorite people by your bed .... thoughts of them will be with you day & night. Put them in pretty Frames.

Pile on the Pillows ~ so inviting!

How romantic ~ a grouping of white **candles** all aglow in the bedroom.

Buy the best quality bed **linens** you can afford ~ they last a long time ... and just think how much time you spend in bed! (Don't you deserve the best & softest?)

Make a unique **headboard** for your bed with flea-market-finds : old porch posts, a mantel, old window or shutters.

Fresh Flowers are a luxurious touch.

Put a dimmer switch on your **bedroom light** for instant ambiance.

O bed! O bed! delicious bed! That heaven on earth to the weary head!
~ Thomas Hood

Bedtime Book Caddy

So simple to make, so handy to use

1. Get a pretty bath towel.

2. Fold bottom upwards about 10" or so.

3. Sew each side edge of towel to secure edges together, like so. → Leave top of "pouch" unsewn.

4. Now, slip the top edge of the towel between your bed's mattress & box springs at the side, right below your pillow. Secure with 3 big safety pins.

Now you have a place to slip your book & glasses when you're ready to sleep!

The Haven:
MY Dream BEDROOM

The perfect little "nest" would have...

canopy bed with 3 mattresses and 17 gorgeous pillows for comfort

a tiny refrigerator hidden under the bedside table, filled with chilled bottles of water & fresh strawberries

a beautiful upholstered chair & ottoman for reading in private

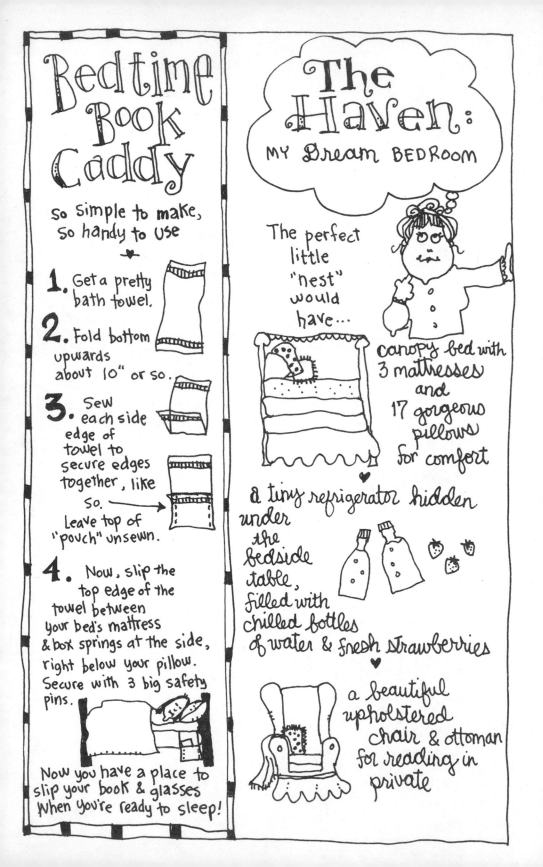

A Warm and Bright Home: LITTLE IDEAS

SCARED OF THE DARK?
JUST A LITTLE?
Tiny white Christmas lights in a ficus tree make a charming night light and scare away boogie men.

MAKE A DRAFT DODGER FOR THE CHILLY WINDOWSILL IN A SNAP!

CUT ONE LEG OUT OF A PAIR OF LITTLE GIRL'S WINTER TIGHTS. FILL THE "LEG" WITH RICE OR DRIED BEANS, AND TIE EACH END WITH A BRIGHT RIBBON. USE FABRIC SQUEEZE-BOTTLE PAINT TO DECORATE THE DRAFT DODGER, OR SEW ON A VARIETY OF CHEERY BIG BUTTONS FOR TRIM.

Be it ever so mortgaged, there's no place like home.

~SAYING ON OLD POSTCARD~

Come to the table
and
Share with me
cookies,
warm gingerbread
and
chamomile tea.

COZY
KitcHen
SAMPLeR

QUICK TO MAKE * CHARMING TO HANG
RIGHT WHERE FRIENDS GATHER

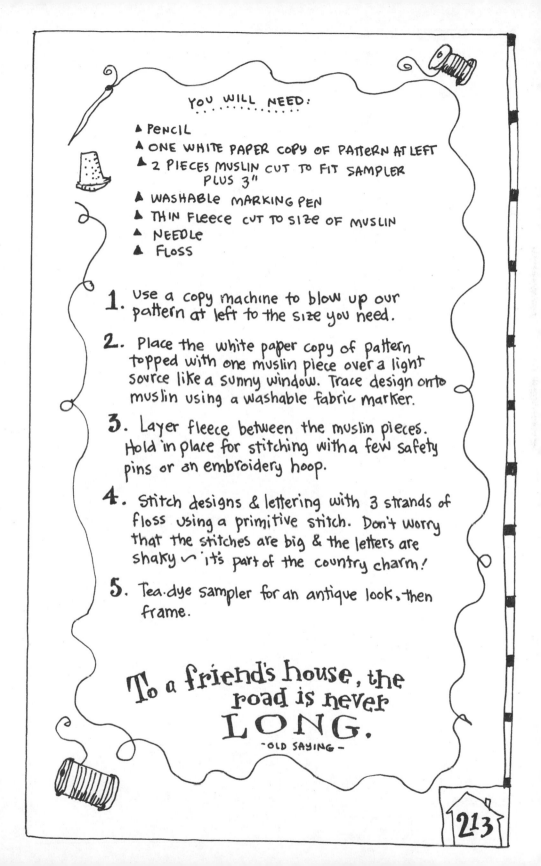

YOU WILL NEED:

▲ PENCIL
▲ ONE WHITE PAPER COPY OF PATTERN AT LEFT
▲ 2 PIECES MUSLIN CUT TO FIT SAMPLER PLUS 3"
▲ WASHABLE MARKING PEN
▲ THIN FLEECE CUT TO SIZE OF MUSLIN
▲ NEEDLE
▲ FLOSS

1. Use a copy machine to blow up our pattern at left to the size you need.

2. Place the white paper copy of pattern topped with one muslin piece over a light source like a sunny window. Trace design onto muslin using a washable fabric marker.

3. Layer fleece between the muslin pieces. Hold in place for stitching with a few safety pins or an embroidery hoop.

4. Stitch designs & lettering with 3 strands of floss using a primitive stitch. Don't worry that the stitches are big & the letters are shaky ~ it's part of the country charm!

5. Tea-dye sampler for an antique look, then frame.

To a friend's house, the road is never LONG.

- OLD SAYING -

213

GrEAT Gifts for a House-Warming

a candle

a wreath

a new broom

a wrought iron hearth cricket

a basket of fruit (don't forget the pineapple)

a loaf of bread

Have a House-Blessing

SPOT

... a great way to make a house a home!

This is fun to do even if you've lived in your house for a long time. A celebration of family & friends, a house blessing can be a religious occasion or just a gathering of good wishes.

Gather family & friends together. Each person may want to bring a poem, quotation or memory of the house to share. Sit or stand in a circle and offer blessings for the house & home, then offer a toast to home owners ...and guests!

"Home sweet home!"
— Holly

Various Blessings
from the Country Friends:

"The beauty of the house is order, the blessing of the house is contentment; the glory of the house is hospitality."
— MARY ELIZABETH

"It takes a heap o' living to make a house a home."
— VICKIE, QUOTING EDGAR GUEST

"May your fridge be full of pudding, your oven full of cookies, and your home full of love."
— Kate

215

♡ TEN TINY TOUCHES
TO MAKE
YOUR HOME

Snug as a bug in a rug!

I JUST LOVE TO SAY THAT.

1. A PICKET FENCE HUGS YOUR HOUSE. Even a little fenced-in herb garden in the backyard is cozy.

2. A BELL BY THE BACK DOOR IS HOMEY. Not a doorbell, mind you,...a bell with a clanger!

3. A BRIGHT BRAIDED RUG AT THE ENTRY SAYS, "THIS IS A COUNTRY HOUSE."

4. A QUILT OVER A TABLE WARMS A ROOM.

5. mommy's MEATLOAF

FRAME A RECIPE HANDWRITTEN BY YOUR MOM OR GRANDMOTHER. Hang it over the stove for a heart-warmer.

6.

A BIG BASKET BY THE DOOR OUT ON THE PORCH IS A CHARMER. Fill it with something unexpected: red Jonathan apples in fall, potatoes in winter.

7.

AN UNCURTAINED WINDOW FESTOONED WITH A ROPE OF CRANBERRIES OR A GARLAND OF DRIED APPLE SLICES IS A CHEERY VIEW.

8.

MONOGRAMS ON YOUR PILLOWCASES DON'T COST MUCH BUT MAKE YOU FEEL LIKE A MILLIONAIRE!

9.

LANTERNS FILLED WITH CITRONELLA OIL WILL GLOW THIS SUMMER. Hang 'em on your porch or deck for beautiful soft lighting.

10.

2 POTTY

A SIMPLE MAT WITH AN EVER-CHANGING PIECE OF ARTWORK BY YOUR KID WILL MAKE A MASTERPIECE FOR YOUR REFRIGERATOR.

The happiest moments in my life have been the few that I passed at home in the bosom of my family. ~ THOMAS JEFFERSON

The fireside is the tulip-bed of a winter day.

– PERSIAN PROVERB –

COLD HANDS, WARM HEART.

Fill your non-working fireplace with a collection of candles for a cozy hearth.

Don't forget to decorate your hearth in the summer:

★ A copper boiler full of birch or white-washed logs is pretty in a summer firebox.

★ A small child's antique chair & raggedy old doll might find a summertime home in a clean fireplace.

★ An old red coaster wagon filled with ferns or bears looks mighty sweet on the hearth during the warm months.

Live your life while you have it. Life is a splendid gift ∽ there is nothing small about it.

∼Florence Nightengale∼

Index

notes

notes

We've cooked up a whole collection of Gooseberry Patch® books!

Have a taste for more? Call us toll-free at
1-800-854-6673

We'll send you our latest catalog filled with snowmen, Santas, ornaments, candles, cookie cutters, gourmet goodies, salt-glazed pottery collectibles and MORE...including our best-selling cookbooks!

Phone us:
1·800·854·6673

Fax us:
1·740·363·7225

Visit our website:
www.gooseberrypatch.com

Send us your favorite recipe!

and the memory that makes it special for you! * We're putting together a brand new **Gooseberry Patch** cookbook, and you're invited to participate. If we select your recipe, your name will appear right along with it...and you'll receive a FREE copy of the book! Mail to:

Vickie & Jo Ann
Gooseberry Patch, Dept. BOOK
P.O. Box 190
Delaware, Ohio 43015

*Please help us by including the number of servings and all other necessary information!

notes